D1188042

NO ORDINARY WAR

NO ORDINARY WAR

THE EVENTFUL CAREER OF U-604

CHRISTIAN PRAG

Dedication

Dedicated to those always at sea,
who found their final resting place in the dark depths of the Atlantic

Frontispiece: The bridge watch of *U-604* at work on stormy seas

Copyright © Christian Prag 2009
Translated from the German by Lawrence Paterson
Translation © Seaforth Publishing 2009

First published in Great Britain in 2009 by
Seaforth Publishing
An imprint of Pen & Sword Books Ltd
47 Church Street, Barnsley
S Yorkshire S70 2AS

www.seaforthpublishing.com
Email info@seaforthpublishing.com

British Library Cataloguing in Publication Data
A CIP data record for this book is available from the British Library

ISBN 978–1–84832–022–2

All rights reserved. No part of this publication may be reproduced
or transmitted in any form or by any means, electronic or mechanical,
including photocopying, recording, or any information storage
and retrieval system, without prior permission in writing
of both the copyright owner and the above publisher.

The right of Christian Prag to be identified as the author
of this work has been asserted by him in accordance with the
Copyright, Designs and Patents Act 1988.

Typeset by Palindrome
Printed in Great Britain by the MPG Books Group

Contents

The only thing that frightened me during the entire war, were the periscopes of the German submarines – and the spirit of their crews – unbroken up to the end.

Winston Churchill

Foreword

This book follows the fate of the German combat U-boat *U-604* which operated in the Atlantic during World War II from the time of its maiden voyage to its sinking in August 1943. Using eyewitness accounts, logbook entries and technical data from the boat's six war patrols, an authentic account of the U-boat war in all its vicissitudes has been provided.

To me it was important to understand all aspects of the history of a combat U-boat in order to form a clear picture of the U-boat war. Each individual boat made up just a small part of the jigsaw puzzle that was the battle of the Atlantic, but concentrating on the fate of a single boat allows us to see what life was like on board: the crew's state of mind and motivation, the complex daily duty structures, battles, boredom, anxiety and courage. These are aspects that publications dealing with the strategy and tactics of the U-boat war are often unable to explore.

Who were the men that fought inside the steel tubes despite no doubt knowing their chances of survival were slim? What drove them, and how did they deal with the endless waiting between battles? What did they do with their free time? How did they live in such close quarters and yet so isolated? This book attempts to answer these questions by following the complete history of *U-604* from the laying of its keel to its scuttling and the tragic return journey of its surviving crew; it is hoped that it will fill the gap in so much related literature.

I came across the powerful story of *U-604* by chance. In 1997 I was fortunate enough to meet a survivor from this boat: I heard the first-hand history of it and to see his private photo collections was fascinating. This fascination was, of course, not only for the fate of the boat itself but for its entire crew.

During the last two years research in archives and contact with other surviving crew members and their opponents from the Allied side have made it possible to show many facets of this brutal war, not just the boat's story but how the humans aboard lived and died.

Christian Prag, Stuttgart

Acknowledgements

M y greatest thanks go to my parents, who encouraged me to write this book. For his tremendous help with the production of this book I would especially like to thank Herr Georg Seitz, who placed a large amount of data and photographs at my disposal as a former member of *U-604*'s crew. Likewise huge thanks to Herr Robert Marquardt and Herr Ernst Winter, who also showed me an abundance of documents from their service days aboard *U-604* which helped in the construction of this book. For the information related to Herr Fritz Wagenführ I am deeply indebted to Gudrun Strüber. For the friendly assistance with further photographs I would like to thank Johanna von Voss.

Thanks are also due to the former crew member of *U-96*, Herr Hermann Friedrich for his photographs of that boat. Help with pictorial material related to the aircraft and base at Natal, Brazil, was given by Mr A. Wilson for which I would like to extend many thanks. For help during the identification of many U-boats within photographs I would especially like to thank Dr Peter Schenk and Dr Axel Niestlé. From the naval archives of the Württembergischen Landes-bibliothek I would like to acknowledge the help of Herr Weis who willingly answered my myriad questions – often unusual ones – related to naval history. Huge thanks also to Herr Horst Bredow of the U-Boot Archive, Altenbruch, for his friendly help with pictorial and other material. From the Federal Archives (Bundesarchiv) I would especially like to thank Herr Erdmann who helped me research documents related to *U-604*. For information related to the Blohm & Voss shipyard I am deeply indebted to Herr Grotz and Herr Kettner of the Thyssen Krupp Marine Systems. Large thanks also to Frau Irene Püttner who always helped with picture enquiries at the Deutsche Museum in Munich. For permission to publish pictures and for quick replies to queries related to these pictures I would also like to thank the team at the American National Archives and Record Administration.

For the collected information on ships sunk by *U-604* I would like to thank

Herr Bernhard Schlummer who cordially allowed me to use his data. I would like to extend many thanks to Captain Henry Helgensen and Herr Archibald Tetzlaff for their help with photographs and information regarding the tragic sinking of the *Coamo*.

Huge thanks are due to Captain Jerry Mason who contributed much data in reference to the final war patrol made by *U-604* and thus was of great assistance to me. Likewise, Herr Peter Binnefeld whose father was a crewman aboard *U-604* and who is very familiar with the history of the boat. Herr Binnefeld helped me with questions about *U-604* and then checked the book for me. For friendly help regarding the air attacks on *U-604* off the Brazilian coast I would like to thank Mr Alan C. Carey. For verifying my information on the sixth war patrol made by *U-604* I would like to offer many thanks to Herr Heinz Trompelt who was a crew member aboard *U-172* at that time.

Many thanks also to Herr Klaus Mattes and Harald Bendert for their support and advice regarding aspects of the publishing business, and to Freya Alexander and Sven Scherer for contributing illustrations of the U-boats. For examining the manuscript and reworking it as necessary I would also like to thank Judith Rau and Karin Wurm. For translation of the book into English and for ideas about the completion of the book I would like to thank Lawrence Paterson. For questions regarding copyright I would very much like to thank Professor Dr Jürgen Rohwer and Herr Jak Mallmann Showell. For very kind cooperation and assistance with Seaforth Publishing I would like to extend large thanks to Robert Gardiner. Finally, a huge thanks to Herr Darko Pelikan and Herr Lorenz Fellmann, who during my research always opened my eyes to the epoch in which I really live.

Introduction

The Allied Convoy System

The prime target for German U-boats was the Allied convoy traffic that stretched between the USA and Great Britain, aiming to prevent the transport of supplies and war materials. But why fight an opponent before it can use such supplies and military materials against the Axis powers on the European continent? The advantage of the tactic is clear: it is far easier to sink a single ship carrying, for example, twenty-five tanks than to destroy those twenty-five tanks on a European battleground. With regards to fuel, a similar logic applies: an enemy machine, whether aircraft, armoured vehicle or ship, is useless without fuel. From these basic strategic principles it could be seen that enemy merchant shipping was a more useful U-boat target than hostile warships. Thus the Axis powers used the principle of blockading the enemy with U-boats, while the Allies had successfully developed their own blockade of the Axis, but using surface vessels.

These different methods of blockade show the U-boat as the weapon of the underdog. It is the role of the inferior navy to attempt supremacy from a hidden vantage point rather than on the open battlefield that navies had traditionally fought over. It is not possible to fight an enemy that you cannot see. Thus a huge expenditure of resources was required by the superior opponent in order to attempt to deal with the submerged threat, binding forces to the hunt for U-boats that could have otherwise been used elsewhere. In order to reduce the vulnerability of individual freighters, Allied merchant shipping formed convoys for crossing the Atlantic, guarded by armed escort ships and aircraft. To balance this, the Germans formed groups of U-boats to make a coordinated attack. This tactic was known as the *Rudeltaktik*, popularised in English history books as the Wolf Pack. But the general situation gradually became unfavourable for U-boats, so that eventually the hunters became the prey. It transpired that Allied aircraft would ultimately become the primary threat to U-boats, not the expected destroyers and security vessels that safeguarded the Allied convoys.

Balance Sheet of the U-boat War in the Second World War

During the Second World War Axis U-boats sank 3,143 ships, totalling 15,865,453 GRT (Gross Registered Tons, in German BRT or *Bruttoregistertonne*). Germany had 1,170 U-boats in service between 1935 and 1945, from which 859 sailed on war patrols. Of these, 630 never returned. 429 boats were declared as confirmed losses, 215 were lost on their first patrols.[1]

From approximately 40,000 German U-boat men 30,000 would never return. No other armed service had a higher casualty rate.

In plain English: of every four outgoing U-boats, only one would return.

But this tragedy was no less on the opposing side. Thousands of sailors lost their lives in the Atlantic sea-lanes.

German U-boats of World War II

Germany began World War II with a multitude of U-boat types that had substantially strengthened technical developments made during the previous war. They were, however, not revolutionary new types, but rather evolutionary developments of the U-boats from World War I.

However, unlike the boats of World War I they had a multiplicity of technical innovations that increased the efficiency. Nonetheless almost throughout the World War II, German U-boats were still merely submersibles, not submarines in the sense that they are known today, that is, able to remain submerged for months. A primary reason for this limitation on submerged travel was the reliance on battery power for the boats' electric drive, which required recharging using the main diesel engines which could only be operated while surfaced. Thus underwater endurance was sharply limited and U-boats operated nearly 90 per cent of the time on the surface. The relatively small power capacity of the lead-acid batteries carried aboard conventional U-boats also limited underwater range. While travelling submerged, the boats themselves could not even at maximum speed hope to escape a hostile destroyer. Only by continuous course and depth changes could surface pursuit be avoided. Thus, submerging served only as an attack or retreat strategy. The boats also required constant modification to counter the dynamics of Allied Antisubmarine Warfare (ASW) developments. This mutual development and counter-development persisted right until the war's end. Hence the following section can serve as merely a rough overview of the most important U-boat types which were used during *U-604*'s active service.

The Type IIA U-boat

Max. diving depth	120 m
Fuel capacity	11.61 tons
Diving time	25–35 seconds
Displacement	surfaced 254 BRT
	submerged 303 BRT
Dimensions	40.9 m × 4.1 m × 3. 8m
Propulsion	two diesels providing 700 hp
	two electric motors providing 360 hp
Maximum speed	surfaced 13 knots
	submerged 6.9 knots
Range	surfaced 1,600 nautical miles at 8 knots
	submerged 35 nautical miles at 4 knots
Torpedo tubes	3 in bow
Torpedoes	5 torpedoes
Deck guns	2 cm flak
Crew strength	25 men

This U-boat type was the first constructed in Germany after the end of World War I. Apart from the small one- and two-man machines later developed, this was the smallest U-boat type that saw active service.

Its size and limited endurance was a hindrance and the reason why the boat was soon replaced at the front and relegated to school training. However, they did continue to see some action both in the Baltic and Black Seas.

The Type VIIC (including U-604)

Max. diving depth	150–180 m
Fuel capacity	113.5 tons
Diving time	25–30 seconds
Displacement	surfaced 769 BRT
	submerged 871 BRT

Dimensions	66.5 m × 6.2 m × 4.74 m
Propulsion	two diesels providing 3,200 hp
	two electric motors providing 750 hp
Maximum speed	surfaced 17.6 knots
	submerged 7.6 knots
Range	surfaced 8,500 nautical miles at 10 knots
	submerged 80 nautical miles at 4 knots
Torpedo tubes	4 in bow, 1 in stern
Torpedoes	14 torpedoes
Deck guns	88 mm deck gun, plus flak weapons
Crew strength	44 men

The development of the type VII U-boat took place between the First and Second World Wars despite U-boat construction being forbidden by the Versailles Treaty. Nonetheless the two shipbuilders, Schürer and Techel, launched the first type VII 12 August 1936. During the war about 700 boats were constructed, making it the most common submarine design of all time. This rate of construction was primarily in proportion to the demands of the convoy war in the North Atlantic and therefore the type VII became the workhorse of the German U-boat fleet.

The Type IXC/40

Max. diving depth	150 m
Fuel capacity	214 tons
Diving time	25–35 seconds
Displacement	surfaced 1,120 BRT
	submerged 1,232 BRT
Dimensions	76.7 m × 6.86 m × 4.67 m
Propulsion	two diesels providing 4,400 hp
	two electric motors providing 1,000 hp
Maximum speed	surfaced 18.2 knots
	submerged 7.7 knots
Range	surfaced 13,850 nautical miles at 10 knots
	submerged 63 nautical miles at 4 knots
Torpedo tubes	4 in bow, 2 in stern

Torpedoes	22 torpedoes
Deck guns	105 mm deck gun, plus flak weapons
Crew strength	49 men

More than 200 type IX U-boats were constructed, making it the second most common type in the German U-boat fleet. It was larger than the type VII and had a much increased radius of action, thus allowing it much longer at sea or to operate in much more remote locations without refuelling. Such a large radius of action would still be considered unusual by today's standards for conventional diesel submarines. This ability was also why these boats were sometimes used as auxiliary supply vessels, as well as journeying as far as Penang in Malaya, or even Japan itself.

However, its size, the type IX made it less agile than the type VIIC, and so too ponderous for the rough-and-tumble of fighting escort vessels. Therefore these boats tended to operate in remote regions where ASW forces were fewer and merchant ships still sailed individually. The commanders for these boats were generally older and with more experience than those who captained the type VIICs, since the large cruiser U-boats required longer to extract themselves from dangerous situations.

The Type XIV

Displacement	surfaced 1,688 BRT
	submerged 1,932 BRT
Dimensions	67.1 m × 9.35 m × 6.51 m
Propulsion:	two diesels providing 2,800 hp
	two electric motors providing 750 hp
Maximum speed	surfaced 14.4 knots
	submerged 6.2 knots
Range	surfaced 12,350 nautical miles at 10 knots
	submerged 55 nautical miles at 4 knots
Torpedo tubes	none
Deck guns	flak weapons
Crew strength	53 men

The type XIV U-boat was designed to supply combat boats with fuel, munitions, spare parts and provisions. Hence crewmen aboard these boats came to know them lovingly as the *Milchkuh*, or 'Milk Cow'. They also carried an onboard doctor, something most combat boats were unable to accommodate. They could also even rotate spare crewmen from the supply boat to replace crewmen killed or incapacitated aboard combat boats.

Without supply U-boats the type VIICs would not have been able to operate off the American or Brazilian coasts. Thus Allied planners made it a priority to sink all of the supply U-boats that they could find, their sole means of defence being flak weapons. The size of the type XIV made it vulnerable to attack. Their casualty rate bears this out: all boats of this type were sunk.

This was not the sole reason that service aboard the type XIV was unpopular with U-boat men. There was no chance of sinking enemy ships, since their role was to bolster the successes of the combat boats through their resupply missions.

The Commander of U-604

The commander of *U-604*, Horst Höltring, was born in Altona, Hamburg, on 30 June 1913, and was already married by the time of the outbreak of World War II. He was a member of the Crew Year 1933 and had reached the rank of Kapitän-leutnant on 1 May 1941. During his career he had served as navigator in the naval air arm on the Ar 197 biplane destined for seervice aboard the *Graf Zeppelin* Germany's first, but never completed, aircraft carrier. However, when con-struction of the carrier was halted he transferred to the U-boat service.

His first command was aboard *U-149*, a small coastal type II boat. Höltring commanded this boat between 13 November 1940 to 30 November 1941. During this period he sank a Soviet submarine, *M-101*, in the Baltic northwest of Dagö Island (59°20' North and 21°12' East) on 26 June 1941.

M-101 had been built in Leningrad, launched in 1939. The small Soviet sub-marine had a displacement tonnage of 261 tons, and was attached to Reval's 1st Submarine Brigade. It was returning from patrol to its base when *U-149* attacked, the entire twenty-strong crew of *M-101* going with their boat to the depths.[2]

On 8 January 1942 the 28-year-old Kapitänleutnant Höltring was appointed as commander of *U-604*, a post he held until its scuttling on 11 August 1943.

The war diary from *U-604* shows the care that Kapitänleutnant Höltring took in his command. He took no unnecessary risks and consequently his crew were never placed in needless risk either. Naturally, this resulted in a positive response from the crew, who felt that Höltring would always return them safely to harbour.

It was only in his use of radio communication that Höltring underestimated danger. When a U-boat sent radio signals, it could be detected by Allied Huff-

Kapitänleutnant Horst Höltring, commander of *U-604*.

Duff (High Frequency/Direction Finding) which would reveal the boat's position so it could be targeted and sunk. Kapitänleutnant Höltring had received his communications training as a navigator while part of the naval aviation arm. In that service an aircraft could cover an enormous distance before Allied direction finding could locate it. By contrast a U-boat behaved very differently: once discovered it could only escape by submerging.

But above all, Höltring was not a commander with a 'sore throat'. This was the name in U-boat jargon for a captain eager for the Knight's Cross. For this decoration many commanders risked all. To qualify for the award a commander initially had to sink 100,000 tons of enemy shipping. Many crews of other boats whose commanders were judged to suffer from 'sore throats' had no confidence that they would return from war patrol.

However, by nature Höltring was a restless, fidgety person. This restlessness would particularly manifest itself in precarious or dangerous situations, which is

U-149 in Wilhelmshaven in 1945. This boat was Kapitänleutnant Höltring's first command
(With kind permission of the Bibliothek für Zeitgeschichte)

perhaps understandable if we could place ourselves in the role of a U-boat commander. He alone was responsible for the fate of the entire crew. He alone must decide in the blink of an eye how to deal with any situation that arises. And it was he who had to answer for the leadership of his U-boat, and unfortunately evaluation of his leadership, as we shall see later, was not always positive.

The psychological strain on a commander was enormous. For example the commander of *U-109*, Bleichrodt, communicated his decision to withdraw from command of his boat during a war patrol. After several radio communications with BdU (*Befehlshaber der U-Boote* – U-boat Command) it was decided that his command be handed to the boat's first watch officer (1 WO) for the remaining patrol. A more extreme form of psychological breakdown resulted in suicide. On 23 October 1943 the commander of *U-505*, Kapitänleutnant Zschech took his own life during a depth-charge attack. He shot himself in the head with his service pistol. *U-505*, a type IXC U-boat, is today a museum exhibit in Chicago. The commander of *U-231*, Kapitänleutnant Wolfgang Wenzel, also tried to shoot himself, but did not die, the bullet remaining lodged in his back.[3] These reactions reflect the enormous pressure on U-boat commanders responsible for a fifty-man crew.

Kapitänleutnant Höltring has been characterised variously in several previous publications. One describes how he shot himself in the toe with his service pistol while drunk, thereby hindering his naval career. Most descriptions portray him as weapon-mad. However, I cannot confirm this characterisation after much research and speaking to eyewitnesses of the time. It seems to me natural that while ashore he carried his service pistol, not just because of the war situation but

M-117 of the Malyutka class, a sister ship for *M-101* that Höltring in *U-149* sank on 26 June 1941

also on account of the fact that he was stationed in an occupied country.

Despite his caution in operations, Höltring could not escape his fate. When, on his last war patrol, his crew were distributed between *U-172* and *U-185* for return to port, Höltring went aboard *U-185*, under Kapitänleutnant Maus. This boat in turn was attacked by aircraft on 24 August 1943 and was so heavily damaged that the crew and survivors from *U-604* were forced to abandon ship. While the boat was sinking Kapitänleutnant Höltring in the bow room decided on suicide and shot himself in the head.

The crew of U-604

The crew of *U-604* came together from all over Germany, as soon as the boat was commissioned. Every recruit had had to complete the same basic U-boat training. Their training started with normal infantry drill and standard naval exercises. For this two training regiments (*Schiffstammregimenten*) had been established by 1938, totalling fourteen separate units. These had acquired various training bases that were numbered and spread along the Baltic (odd numbers) and North Sea (even numbers) coasts. In these bases recruits underwent basic training which could last up to six months.[4]

The path that a recruit's training followed depended primarily on the selected career. If he selected the U-boats then he would, of course, be examined for fitness specifically for service within the U-boats. If the recruit passed this stage then U-boat training would begin, if not then he was destined for service either in the surface fleet or ashore.

Many books have stated that U-boats were manned by volunteers, though this was often not the case. Frequently men were transferred without their fore-knowledge or choice into the U-boat service; they simply became U-boat crew whether they had wished to or not. However, there were additional rewards for this branch of the navy, one of which was financial. Many regarded attachment to U-boat as beneficial as they received extra pay to the normal rate, including 'machine pay' and 'tropical pay' for when the boat entered tropical regions in the course of a war patrol. According to statements made by a former crew member of *U-604*, these extra allowances alone were sufficient to keep him content with U-boat service regardless of the often arduous conditions.[5]

Following standard infantry training the sailors destined for U-boat service were transferred to a submarine training division (*Unterseeboots-Lehrdivision,* ULD) where proper U-boat training began. Here men were divided into their prospective roles aboard the U-boats. Future machinists were assigned to the 1st ULD in Pillau. There, since there was insufficient space in both the accom-modation and classrooms ashore for the constant influx of recruits, the 'Strength Through Joy' cruise ship *Robert Ley* was commandeered, used as a floating barracks and training centre as it lay in Pillau harbour.

11th Schiffsstammabteilung in Stralsund, 1939

A recruit's wardrobe

The *Robert Ley* was sister ship to the *Wilhelm Gustloff*, launched in 1938 and beginning work as a cruise liner. At the outbreak of war it was converted into a hospital ship and served in this role until the end of 1939. It served as attachment to the 1st ULD as accommodation until the middle of 1944 when it again reverted to the role of hospital ship, evacuating wounded and refugees in the Baltic from the approaching Russians. The ship's end was in Hamburg harbour where it was bombed and burnt out by the Royal Air Force. In 1947 it took its final voyage when it was towed as a wreck to England and scrapped.

Future radio personnel and men destined for the Seaman's branch aboard the U-boats were posted to the 2nd ULD in Gotenhafen. There lay the other 'Strength Through Joy' cruise ship, the *Wilhelm Gustloff*, in harbour that was, like the *Robert Ley*, used as barracks for the recruits in U-boat training.

The *Wilhelm Gustloff* was launched in 1937 from the Blohm & Voss shipyard in Hamburg. After a single cruise the liner was also converted to a hospital ship

Recruits training in Stralsund, 1939

The first day's liberty after six weeks of infantry training

Swearing the oath in Stralsund 1939

The *Robert Ley*

at the outbreak of war, operating as transport for wounded troops from the Norwegian campaign before moved to Gotenhafen as accommodation ship for 2nd ULD on 20 November 1940.

After its service as an accommodation ship for the 2nd ULD the *Wilhelm Gustloff* was the centre of on the darkest chapters in maritime history. On 30 January 1945 she was torpedoed and sunk by Soviet submarine *S-13* while evacuating refugees and retreating troops from the eastern Baltic coast as the Russians advanced. There were at least 10,300 people crammed aboard when the Russian torpedoes hit and over 9,000 people went to the bottom with her, not just women and children but 100 U-boat personnel being taken to safety from the training ports under threat by the Russian advance.

The ULD was where the future U-boat men learned the theory and practice of U-boat warfare. For practical training they used the type II U-boats which were the perfect size for this purpose. Though they had been front line U-boats in the early stages of the war they were found to be lacking in the Atlantic convoy battles, so the entire class was relegated to training duties. These boats were so small that their crews named them 'dugout canoes' (*Einbäume*).

Training boats were generally those that had been found to be lacking in the

The *Wilhelm Gustloff*. (With kind permission of Ullstein Bild)

Atlantic battle. For the type II it was their small size and weapon load. But there were also more exotic training boats. For example, there was a single British submarine – the Porpoise Class minelayer HMS *Seal* – which had fallen into German hands on 5 May 1940. The English crew had suffered a massive technical problem which resulted in their surrender to German aircraft. The captured English submarine was incorporated into the Kriegsmarine as *UB* on 30 November 1940. The boat was swiftly relegated to training purposes as its ammunition and spare parts requirement were not compatible with standard German equipment. Commitment to front line service would have required much expense, far beyond the potential benefits and so it served in the training flotillas.

After U-boat training, the new crewmen were then posted to the *Baubelehrung*, a chance to oversee the construction of their U-boat. It was finally at this point that the men learned to which boat they had been assigned. During this period the crew had a chance to familiarise themselves with their new U-boat and the other men that would sail alongside them. They were also able to receive further

Above: U-boat training aboard the *Wilhelm Gustloff* 1941. Here the recruits are practising knot-tying. Third from right is the future Funkmaat from *U-604*, Georg Seitz. *Left*: Matrose Georg Seitz in his white uniform photographed prior to the war in 1939.

instruction from the shipyard personnel as well as other crewmen. The average age of *U-604*'s crew was, as far as records show, 21.5 years. While this at first sounds very young, it was nothing compared to later in the war when the high casualty rate led to an even younger average age for U-boat crews. A prime example of this was *U-955*, eventually captained by a 21-year-old commander.[6] But in 1940 these conditions had not yet arisen when *U-604*'s crew finally convened at their U-boat, which was still under construction. The crew roster would change before each patrol as men were posted to further training courses between each sailing, the Wachoffiziere (watch officers) in particular changing as men were promoted on their way toward commands of their own.

From Building Yard to the First War Patrol

On 22 May 1940 the Blohm & Voss shipyard in Hamburg received the building contract for *U-604*. It was to be a type VIIC U-boat, the workhorse of the U-boat service. Blohm & Voss had an excellent reputation for shipbuilding, many U-boat crewmen stating that they believed that they built the best boats.[7]

However, Blohm & Voss were not the only company that constructed U-boats. This was not just the bitter necessity imposed by severe U-boat losses in the Atlantic. The average construction period of a VIIC amounted to about nine months. Construction was spread between the following shipyards: Blohm & Voss, Bremen Vulkan, Danziger Werft, Deschimag Atlas, Deutsche Werft, Deutsche Werke, Elbing, Flensburger Schiffbau, Germaniawerft, Howaldswerke, Kriegsmarine (KMW), Lübecker Flenderwerke, Neptune, Nordseewerke, Reichswerft Danzig, Seebeck, Stettiner Oderwerke, Schichau, Stülcken and Vulkan. On 27 February 1941, one month after the contract for *U-604* was issued under the build number 104, and her keel was laid in Hamburg. At the beginning of construction work only shipyard workers were involved but as the boat slowly took shape Chief Engineer Jürgens and his engineering personnel started to familiarise themselves with the boat, so the technical crew were able to obtain a good overall picture of the construction progress. They were instructed on all aspects of their boat's construction by the shipyard engineers.

The boat's crew was not yet in charge of their own boat. Only slowly were more personnel added to the roster of men observing the construction process of *U-604*. This gradual process educated the crew about all the details of the boat in regard to their assigned station aboard. It was only in the final stages of construction that it was possible for the men to study all the technical equipment and its installation as once completed they would more often than not be obscured behind pipes, cables and hull lining.

On 16 November 1941 the boat was successfully launched. Following this

The Blohm & Voss shipyard. In the foreground there are several U-boats under construction. (With kind permission of Thyssen Krupp Marine Systems)

Left: A segment of the 22 mm strong pressure hull is lifted by crane into the nearly completed hull of a type VII boat. *Right*: A type VII in the Blohm & Voss yard.(With kind permission of Thyssen Krupp Marine Systems)

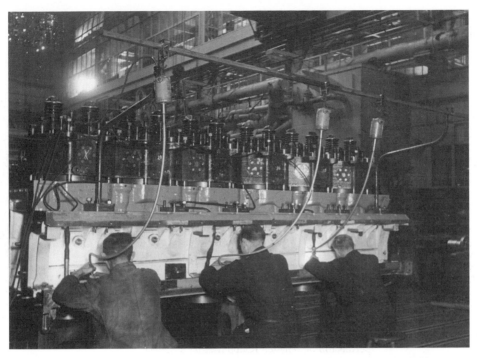

Above: Shipyard workers on the Blohm & Voss production line installing components for the U-boats' construction. *Below*: Yard workers on a type VII in the Blohm & Voss yards.
(With kind permission of Thyssen Krupp Marine Systems)

The elegant tapered bow of a type VII U–boat.
(With kind permission of Thyssen Krupp Marine Systems)

A shipyard worker working on a type VII U-boat. He is riveting deck plating in place.
(With kind permission of Thyssen Krupp Marine Systems)

highly symbolic moment, further work was undertaken on the boat. Over the next day, the yard workers tested the boat and presented their results to the U-boat Acceptance Command – *U-Boot-Abnahme-Kommando* (UAK).

The UAK took the boat over for more work and tests on the machinery, hydroplanes and helm. In the meantime the entire crew had been assembled, although it was only after release from the UAK that *U-604* was able to join the 5th U-Flotilla in Kiel on 8 January 1942.

Training began one day after commissioning. For U-boat crews this generally meant that each man learned the basics of the other men's stations, so that every man could fill in at a moment's notice almost any post aboard the boat. However, *U-604* was only afforded the opportunity to train for its immediate front-line service. Few of the instructors on hand had experienced combat, as veterans were sorely needed at the front as the ultimate success of the U-boat war hung in the balance. Some of *U-604*'s crew had seen action on previous war patrols aboard other boats, their experiences invaluable to fresh recruits who relished the opportunity to learn from those who had first-hand experience. In the case of future emergencies every man needed to be able to rely on all others; an incorrect decision possibly spelling death for the entire crew.[8] After several days of successful

Commissioning of *U-604* on 8 January 1942. The crew are assembled on the stern deck.

training on the Elbe, *U-604* sailed for its new flotilla in Kiel.

On 12 January 1942 the boat began its journey along the Kaiser Wilhelm Canal. The canal led past the *Reichskolonialschule* where women were prepared for life in the expanding number of 'colonies' recently occupied by the Wehrmacht. Naturally, shortly before passing the school, *U-604*'s ship's horn was sounded and available crew paraded on deck as the school's women answered in kind.

By the following day *U-604* had reached Kiel and on 14 January came under scrutiny by the UAG – *U-Boot-Abnahmegruppe* – who tested the boat's 'heart and lungs'. The UAG was similar in essence to the UAK but the former also comprised additional officers that had served during the First World War and could bring their combat experience to the fresh sets of tests. These took an average of two weeks, although the inhospitable January weather played its part in extending this period. The port's capacity was reduced by severe icing, the time when *U-604* was unable to move used instead for further onboard training. It was only by 11 February that *U-604*, with the assistance of an ice-breaker, was able to put to sea in order to test the listening gear (*Gruppenhorchgerät* or GHG), the apparatus used to detect ship engine noises while the boat was submerged. The UAG tests continued to be hampered by the severe weather and they were only completed by 20 April as the conditions moderated. Next was transfer to Danzig and the so-called AGRU front (*Ausbildungsgruppe*, training group). During the voyage, which lasted until 23 April, further tests of the boat's machinery were

The crew posing for a group photograph. In the first row, from left to right are: Obersteuermann Finster, Leitender Ingenieur Jürgens, Kommandant Höltring, Wachoffizier Poeschel and Obermaschinist Aloe.

made before arrival in Danzig and commencement of training that more realistically mimicked conditions at the front. There, within the Baltic Sea, *U-604* practised outmanoeuvring convoy escort vessels, penetrating escort screens, torpedo shooting both submerged and surfaced and the art of the crash dive. These exhausting drills were completed by 17 May 1942 and the boat judged nearly ready for combat.

The final stages of training saw *U-604* sailing between Danzig and Gotenhafen attached to the 25th U-Flotilla. Off Bornholm the boat exercised its submerged stalking. The boat was monitored by underwater microphones as it ran submerged on silent routine in order to judge the effectiveness of both boat and crew in this situation – something that could spell life or death in the Atlantic battle. It would be fatal if the U-boat or its complement made any unwanted noises that could allow the enemy to detect their presence.

Further torpedo firing exercises attached to the 25th U-Flotilla were then

33

carried out before the boat sailed for Kiel on 30 June 1942 and finally on to the Blohm & Voss yards in Hamburg. There *U-604* had all the minor technical problems discovered by the UAK and UAG remedied and any accumulated wear and tear dealt with, which included rust treatment, after which the boat began preparations for its first war patrol. Between 25 and 28 July *U-604* had its radio communications systems checked and entered the degaussing range where the magnetic signature of the hull was electronically removed. After a final test of the boat's trim, *U-604* was declared operational. On 3 August 1942 *U-604* ran into Kiel in order to begin its maiden patrol. But the so-called 'Happy Time' of the U-boat crew was over and unbeknownst to the new combat-ready crew what came to be the turning point in the battle of the Atlantic was in actuality mere months away. In fact the lifespan of a combat U-boat was estimated to be as low as sixty-two days at sea by this stage of the war.[9] *U-604* was the 240th combat boat to set sail and it put to sea to enter the grand arena of the battle of the Atlantic as German planners continued to cling to possible victory in the ocean.

The First War Patrol

The first journey for each U-boat was also known as the 'transfer journey' since the boat was moved from its German base to one on the French Atlantic. By this time France has been occupied by the Axis powers who highly valued its Atlantic bases as convenient for attacking Allied convoy traffic. However, the transfer from Germany still required the complicated and dangerous voyage from the North Sea into the Atlantic. The sea area around northern Germany was known to men of the Kriegsmarine as the *Nasse Dreieck* – the wet triangle. It was through this region that *U-604* sailed on its first trip from Kiel to France.

U-boats were unable to traverse the narrow straits that lay between Dover and Calais, which was extremely heavily patrolled and during the First World War had been extensively mined. This mine barrier – the so-called Dover Barrage – had comprised 10,000 mines arranged in deep and shallow fields. The Second War saw more mining of the area by the Royal Navy, whose surface ships scoured the region in search of enemy motor torpedo boats and submarines. Three U-boats were sunk by mines at the war's beginning, so BdU forbade passage of the English Channel en route to France.[10] Since then U-boats had navigated north of Great Britain, traversing the waters off Scotland and entering the North Atlantic by that route.

Before departing Kiel the boat had been completely equipped with additional technical equipment, fuel and provisions. During the equipping of a type VIIC for an operational period of six weeks at sea, provisions alone weighed approximately 4 tons. Every single angle was considered for the provisioning of the boat, a task hampered by the narrowness of the hull. Even the second WC functioned as a storeroom for rations. This demonstrated the very deliberate construction of the U-boat solely as a weapon of war – crew comfort was secondary to its ability to function in combat operations. All other considerations were of lesser importance, hence the use of the toilet as a storeroom, but the crew did not mind. After some time at sea the rations began to taste of diesel oil anyway.

The evening before the boat was due to leave the crew celebrated as if there were be no tomorrow. But, of course, morning dawned as it always did, although the question in many of the newer crewmen's heads was whether there would be only one more morning until they saw of their first war patrol. During my research I asked one of the U-boat men what kind of thoughts ran through his mind prior to sailing and he replied:

> Of course, we were afraid. But we had no choice, we weren't asked whether we wanted to sail or not.

U-604 departed Kiel-Wik on 4 August 1942, bound for the Kiel lightship at 10.42 hours. It was the fifth boat during the month of August to embark on its first operational journey, one of a total of thirty U-boats that would sail into North Atlantic war patrols in August 1942. Of course, *U-604* was one of the minority of boats that began its journey into action from Germany, most of her sister boats putting to sea from the French Atlantic coast where they had already transferred. From the total of thirty boats that sailed in August, a staggering twenty-two were on their first war patrols. From all that sailed, six would fail to return, five of them from their maiden voyage.[11] In return U-boats sank 117 Allied ships totalling 587, 245 BRT. The following month 96 more ships totalling 461, 794 BRT were also to be sunk.[12]

On 4 August 1942 the sea state into which *U-604* sailed was only rated 0 to 1 'as smooth as a duck pond'. But after a while the weather became 'so-so' with cloudy skies and rain showers. The boat arrived at the Kiel lightship at 01.23 hours and anchored in 18 metres of water. There, in what was designated 'Position Red 16', they were to rendezvous with their escort at 20.04 hrs that evening. After this the boat would head into the '*Großer Belt*' (Great Belt) with their escort ship, heading north towards Norway.

The following day *U-604* changed escort vessel at 'Point Red 27'; the new armed trawler a part of the Kristiansand *Sicherungsflottille* (Security Flotilla generally equipped with armed trawlers and converted merchant vessels). *U-604* tied up at Kristiansand's Silo Dock at 05.43 hours on 6 August 1942. Here the boat would be replenished with fresh provisions and water before slipping from harbour the following day and heading under escort for the open sea once more. On the afternoon of 7 August after completing its obligatory test dive, *U-604* dismissed its escort and began its first war patrol proper.

The test dive was a daily routine designed to test the boat's operability while submerged. The weight of the boat changed fractionally with every mile that they travelled. These regular dives allowed the chief engineer to compensate for

Picture taken in the control room of *U-604* during a dive; note the steep dive-angle of the boat.

the variation by the use of special ballast tanks and trimming pumps. The boat also became heavier day by day, and with each nautical mile: the fuel bunkers were open to the sea at the bottom, so that as diesel was used up seawater could enter the tank. Since the seawater was denser than the diesel oil, the oil floated on top of it, but as it increased in volume the boat gained weight. The advantage of this system was that the fuel bunkers did not need to be pressure-resistant as they were always open to the ambient pressure around the boat.

However, the increase in weight meant there was a corresponding decrease in buoyancy. To be compensate for this, special compensating tanks – *Regelzellen* – were used. These were controlled by 1 Zentralemaat Robert Marquardt who provided a daily trimming report which required great experience to do it effectively. For example, as previously mentioned, Marquardt needed an exact report from the *Smutje* (the crew's name for the boat's cook) of how much food had been used and where the remainder was stored on board the boat. Even slight misplacement of stored provisions could have upset the U-boat's trim, causing problems in the course of a dive. Also, the salinity of the surrounding seawater needed to be checked. This was of enormous importance as it affected the boat's buoyancy. In the past it had been found with midget submarines that in the brackish water found inshore the hull would suddenly sink into what were, in effect, patches of less dense fresh water that had run off the land that did not provide sufficient lift for the hull. Once all of these calculations had been made by Marquardt he submitted them to Chief Engineer Jürgens who would verify and sign the report before the compensating tanks were trimmed accordingly. By this complex procedure the safety of the boat while diving could be assured. Naturally the test dives also allowed the boat's outboard vents and valves to be tested though this was of secondary importance.

After its test dive *U-604* steered north into its operational area, a position north of the British Isles, from where they would head west into the Atlantic Ocean. During the following five days *U-604* covered 664.1 nautical miles. This passage was relatively uneventful, except for passing two floating mines, and despite the fact that the boat was forced to operate for a large part submerged due to poor visibility and rain showers.

On 13 August 1942 at 05.51 hours in the morning, a shout rang out from the bridge: 'Strong smoke trail in sight!' However, after an hour of pursuit the chase was broken off when the source revealed itself as a small trawler. Considering the need to conserve fuel *U-604* headed elsewhere. Only one hour later, another shout came from the lookouts: 'Alarm! Aircraft approaching!' The boat had to make its first crash-dive beneath the surface. Now the crew fully understood what needed to be done; the reality of the U-boat war had just hit home.

Once the bridge watch had shouted for the boat to submerge, they had to hurry through the conning tower hatch lest they be caught above deck as it cut under water. They leapt for the ladder that led from the bridge into the control room (*Zentrale*), falling straight down on to the decking below, each successive man either jumping or being pulled aside so that those above did not land on him. The force of the impact on the floor plating was so heavy that they were frequently deformed and had to be repaired before they were too bent out of shape. The diesels were stopped and electric motors engaged and, once all compartments reported ready to submerge, the senior bridge watch officer ordered tanks flooded after closing the heavy conning tower hatch. Hydroplanes were both put to 'hard down' and exhaust vents closed. So as to minimise diving time, all available crew raced through the boat for the bow compartment where their extra weight would help drag the boat's nose underwater. Chief Engineer Jürgens had to carefully monitor the angle at which the boat descended lest it get out of control and the U-boat sink too swiftly into the depths in what could become an unmanageable dive.

There were probably several boats that lost control during crash-dives during the war and thus sank past their maximum depth rating where the extreme water pressure could crush the hull. But the chief engineer on *U-604* understood his job and smoothly controlled the boat's descent. After that it was time to adjust the trimming cells with compressed air. These had been already flooded while travelling surfaced in order to obtain a faster diving time when needed. After this had been done and the dive arrested, the boat was trimmed at a light upward angle so that bubbles which had collected in the corner of the diving tanks could escape. After this manoeuvre Jürgens announced 'Boat level!' and the first alarm dive had been successfully completed. Although the expected air attack with either bombs or depth-charges never materialised, the boat stayed submerged for its own security lest the enemy still be overhead. While travelling submerged U-boats tended to move as slowly as possible as the type VIIC only had a limited range of 80 nautical miles at 4 knots before the batteries would be completely exhausted and the boat forced to surface. It made more physical sense to discharge the batteries slowly in order to extend the possible underwater range. If a greater speed was used, electrolyte in the lead-acid battery would be warmed by the higher current density, resulting in a decreased underwater range. Besides, by heating the electrolyte the battery would age faster and the capacity would decrease even further. For these reasons commanders were urged to use minimal submerged speed where applicable, only using top underwater capability in precarious situations where the boat's survival could depend on rapid changes of direction. *U-604* had obviously escaped the attention of its potential attacker, and an hour later surfaced once more to resume its transit into the Atlantic.

The following day a transformer burned out from to overloading, due partly to a high level of radio traffic. Ironically this technical fault had unforeseen benefits as there was an enforced radio silence on the boat, negating the ability of Allied Huff-Duff to pinpoint the travelling U-boat by homing on its radio traffic to BdU. Thus *U-604*'s position remained unknown to the Allies for the time being.

Huff-Duff was a major Allied technological advance that had begun to be built into escort ships at the beginning of 1942, allowing them roughly to pinpoint German radio transmissions and locate U-boats on patrol. Transmission only seconds long could be enough to betray a U-boat – the Allies were assisted by BdU's insistence on frequent reports on position and patrol status.[13] Although not exact, Huff-Duff was capable of detecting the general area that a U-boat lay in, not only allowing the Allied ships to hunt them but also allowing redirection of convoy traffic away from potential U-boat concentrations. The Germans knew little of the exact nature of the Allied equipment, although naturally rumours and presumptions spread throughout the Kriegsmarine, yet Dönitz never issued official orders that only messages as brief as possible should be transmitted to BdU or other boats in case of enemy interception.

The next day a radio message was received that directed *U-604* to join the group Lohs that was gathering to operate against a convoy sighted by *U-256*

Left: A Huff-Duff antenna onboard an Allied escort vessel. *Right*: A Huff-Duff receiver.
(With kind permission of the Bibliothek für Zeitgeschichte)

commanded by Kapitänleutnant Odo Löwe.

By the beginning of 12 August the Lohs Group consisted of nine boats, stretched in a line south of Iceland. Löwe in *U-256* was, like Höltring in *U-604*, on his first war patrol. The boats travelled at full speed to their allotted patrol zones in order to locate the convoy and its escorts as quickly as possible.

The bridge watch scoured the horizon with their binoculars in search of the enemy escort ships. For these men it was a four-hour shift of intense concentration under very adverse circumstances. It was perfectly valid for these men to use as many of their senses as possible to locate the enemy, including their sense of smell. Previously lookouts on other boats had smelled smoke, the boat steering directly upwind, and actually discovered the convoy escort. The smell of smoke and flame had come from a torpedoed and burning tanker on that occasion. But the lookouts aboard *U-604* could see, smell or hear nothing and so by the evening of the following day, 15 August, the pursuit was broken off. Not only was location proving impossible, but also the weather had deteriorated to a force 4 to 5 and heavy swell that would make surfaced torpedo shooting difficult or unworkable.

During the following day *U-604* completed a test dive and the boat's torpedoes were regulated as well. Only those already loaded into the tubes could undergo this routine maintenance as there was simply no space available to deal with the stored reserve torpedoes. Each torpedo was pulled from its tube: at 711 kilograms, 7 metres in length and 0.533 metres in diameter, it was no wonder that crew regarded this task as heavy labour. To regulate the G7a air-driven torpedo, the stored compressed air needed to be checked and topped up if necessary. This type of torpedo was best used in night attacks, since its propulsion by stored air left a betraying wake behind it in the water and could thus not only warn potential targets of impending danger, but also reveal the boat's position. Torpedoes were highly complex weapon systems and a single G7a could cost 24,000 Reichmarks and took more than 3,000 man-hours to produce.[14] Therefore such maintenance to reduce the possibility of misfire or malfunction was essential aboard the boats. The other type of torpedo, the G7e, was propelled electrically. It contained a lead-acid battery that required maintenance as well; the battery's electrolyte level required checking. Before the torpedo was fired it also had to be preheated, which increased its range by as much as 60 per cent.[15] This preheating reduced the internal resistance within the battery, which rises with falling temperature. Hence the electrical motor could take a larger current flow and improve both speed and range. Despite the need for such a complex procedure, this type of torpedo had the great advantage that it produced less of a wake and thus gave no warning of approach, and did not reveal the attacking U-boat's position.

During this submerged period of travel while the torpedoes were being regulated the crew heard the distinct sound of distant screws. Höltring brought the boat to periscope depth but he could see nothing and ordered *U-604* to surface. A little under fifteen minutes later the source of the sound was observed: an enemy corvette which disappeared into a rain squall at a distance of still 600 metres. The U-boat was able to submerge and creep away undetected. On 16 August the same situation occurred, although this time a steamer was also seen trailing the corvette. *U-604* immediately attached itself to the heels of this small convoy. However, within the hour *U-604* became plagued by mechanical problems; the gyroscope compass failed, a transformer and even the port engine allowing the steamer to slip from sight. *U-604* dived in order to make repairs in the stability of submerged travel.

In addition, these sighting and subsequent problems could not be transmitted to BdU because of the defective transformer in the radio transmitter. Perhaps this actually prevented attack by the enemy corvette as once more its Huff-Duff was ineffectual in the face of enforced radio silence. After the repairs were completed *U-604* surfaced once more and continued to search for targets. But it was not until four days later on 22 August when *U-604* was approximately 1,300 km off the west coast of Ireland that the bridge watch shouted 'Enemy in sight!' *U-604* had found the convoy that had been detected previously and reported by Kapitänleutnant Friedrich Hermann Prätorius. Like *U-604*, *U-135* had been integrated into the Lohs group and now *U-604* took up position outside and ahead of the convoy, running at full speed, but subsequently lost contact in the intermittent rain. For another day Höltring scoured the area to regain contact, but it was not until 18.12 hours on 23 August that *U-135* and *U-373* regained the convoy. Shortly afterwards a third U-boat, *U-660*, transmitted the message that it had also made contact and was beginning operations. Kapitänleutnant Götz Baur in *U-660* was like both Prätorius and Höltring in that this was his boat's first patrol. Höltring, using the beacon signals transmitted from *U-660*, homed in on the convoy until by chance on 24 August, a 12,000-ton unescorted solo-sailing ship hove into view.

Höltring opted to begin action against this single enemy ship at all possible speed. He continued to observe the target while his boat was travelling surfaced by means of the extended periscope. Using this method Höltring could see the tips of the ship's smokestacks while his bridge watch from their lower vantage point were only able to observe the mastheads themselves. Since the moonlight was very bright and almost uninterrupted by the high cloud cover, Höltring decided on a submerged attack. However, the zigzagging steamer foiled his first submerged approach as it changed its general course forcing *U-604* to surface and use its higher speed on diesel engines for the pursuit. By 03.45 hours the boat was in firing position. A three-torpedo salvo was fired when the target was at a range of 1,500 metres. The enemy steamer was so close and large through the targeting optics that only one small portion of it was visible at a time.

A hit was scored amidships, betrayed by a huge column of water alongside the target. Through the listening gear a metallic strike was heard immediately before the explosion, perhaps pointing to a failure in the pistol of the first torpedo fired. The ship lost speed almost immediately and began to heel to starboard. At 03.56 hours a *coup-de-grâce* shot was fired and hit, the steamer leaning first to starboard and later back to port as water poured over the fore ship and she sank into the depths in position 52.05°N, 30.50°W. There then followed two further detonations that were heard, possibly explosions caused by cold water on hot engine parts and the hull cracking under the water pressure as it sunk.

The MV *Abbekerk* was a merchant motor ship of 7,906 BRT travelling from Port of Spain in Trinidad to Liverpool, England. The ship carried 9,489 tons of sugar, mail and other goods aboard. The *Abbekerk* had sailed on 15 August on its voyage to Liverpool and was therefore ten days at sea when she was sunk.

Somewhat ironically perhaps, the ship had been built in Germany by the F.

MV *Abbekerk,* sunk by *U-604* on 25 August 1942.

Schichau GmbH in Danzig for a Dutch ship-owner. She had had an interesting history already, having been sunk once previously by German air attack on 7 July 1940 while anchored in the Thames at London. However, in such shallow water the ship had been easily raised, repaired and sailed once more. In *U-604*'s attack, two men were killed from the sixty-four-man crew; the first mate and the ship's cook. The remaining sixty-two men escaped and saved themselves aboard two lifeboats which they steered in the direction of Ireland. It is somewhat unusual that the survivors had lifeboats and not life rafts as on many ships the latter were considered safer. These were simply laid on the merchant ship and if sunk would float free to the surface, whereas proper lifeboats required careful launching so as not to founder. During the course of a torpedoing there was often not sufficient time to launch such boats and the sailors were forced to cling to whatever buoyant material was available in the water to survive. However, *Abbekerk*'s survivors were fortunate as three days later they were found and rescued by the corvette HMS *Wallflower* from the escort of convoy ON 122.

In view of the fact that the sinking of the *Abbekerk* took place in North Atlantic, it is likely that both lifeboats could not have reached the Irish coast under their own speed. When the rescuing corvette had rejoined the convoy

The corvette HMS *Wallflower* that rescued survivors from the MV *Abbekerk*.
(With kind permission of the Bibliothek für Zeitgeschichte)

escort, the survivors from the Dutch motor vessel were distributed among other ships. After reaching the UK, eighteen of them transferred to the Dutch merchant navy's *Jan van Goyen*. It is probable that the survivors received compensation for their sinking. Although this sounds odd, these payments, called 'torpedo money' in the payments' register, were made whenever a ship was torpedoed, .

After sinking the *Abbekerk*, Höltring reported his success to BdU in accordance with standing orders. The defective coil within the transformer of the radio transmitter had to be cooled using compressed air as the message was sent, in case it burnt ou completely.

U-604 then continued to operate in the *Lohs* group against the target convoy. However, on the following day Höltring received instructions by radio from BdU to discontinue pursuit of that convoy and instead to proceed to naval grid square AK 39. For the purposes of navigation the entire Atlantic had been divided into squares, with letters and numbers that could be coded to give a specific map reference using only a few numerals and letters. Correspondingly the boats in the picket line that stretched between AK 3765 and AK 6629 – an approximate position 1,900 kilometres west of the Scottish coast – were ordered to move onwards. After four further uneventful days, *U-604* was integrated into this group, which was instructed to move in position at midnight on 29 August on a course of 25°, covering an area of 120 nautical miles as they hunted for targets. In this reconnaissance line, known as the Vorwärts group, were the following boats: *U-609* (Rudloff), *U-407* (Brüller), *U-91* (Walkering), *U-411* (Litterscheiderste), *U-92* (Oelrich), *U-659* (Stock), *U-756* (Harney), *U-409* (Massman) and *U-211* (Hause).[16] Remarkably, all of these boats were on their first combat patrols.

On 31 August Rudloff announced that after twenty-five hours of searching, *U-609* had made contact with a convoy in quadrant AK 2914. It was SC 97, a slow-moving convoy bound from Canada to England. *U-604* immediately turned on the assumed general course that the convoy was taking, its exact course not yet determined. Höltring proceeded slowly so as to conserve fuel while the contact boat attempted to establish more precise navigational information.

SC 97 consisted of fifty-eight ships, escorted by the Escort Group C 2 that comprised destroyers HMS *Burnham* and *Broadway* as well as corvettes *Brandon*, *Daulhin*, *Drumheller* and *Morden*.[17]

U-609 attacked immediately and sank the 5,625-ton Panamanian registered SS *Capira* as well as the 4,663-ton Norwegian MV *Bronxville*. At around 17.10 hours on 31 August it was finally *U-604*'s turn as the bridge watch finally sighted the convoy. Höltring ordered full speed as he tried to close the gap to the target. At around 19.05 hours two escort vessels appeared on the horizon and were soon deemed by Höltring to be approaching too close and he ordered an emergency dive and the ejection of a 'Bold' sonar decoy, a chemical compound that created a fine carpet of bubbles in the water to confuse the ASDIC (ultrasonic underwater sound detection, also well known as sonar) reception by hunting enemy warships.

After the screw noises of the approaching warships began to recede once more, *U-604* returned to periscope depth and risked an all-round look, surfacing once the coast appeared to be clear. At around 21.20 hours two hostile corvettes were seen emerging from a rain squall, so Höltring manoeuvred *U-604* out of harm's way while continuing to chase the convoy. It wasn't long until his tactics were rewarded. At 22.25 hours the forward right-hand lookout on *U-604*'s bridge sighted smoke on the horizon and by dawn the boat was firmly attached to the convoy's trail, the merchants clearly visible against the skyline. *U-604*, on the other hand, was against a dark horizon and so well protected from discovery. Since radio silence was still enforced on the boat due to the faulty transformer, neither signals nor beacons could be sent which although rendered them unable to vector other boats on the convoy, also protected them from Huff-Duff location. Thus *U-604* remained undetected, an advantage that Höltring capitalised on.

Three-quarters of an hour past midnight *U-604* mounted an attack on a steamer from the convoy. Although unknown to Höltring, at this time there were six U-boats in contact with SC 97. At 01.55 hours Höltring fired three torpedoes and immediately turned away for a final shot at an estimated 4,000–5,000-ton steamer behind the first target. However, much to Höltring's chagrin, both steamers altered course as part of their irregular zigzag after all torpedoes had been fired, and were thus spared as the shots went wide of their targets. Perhaps in hindsight Höltring should have opted for a four-shot spread against the first steamer rather than splitting his targets, perhaps also spreading the shots wider to cater for a potential change of direction, but this is merely conjecture.

Nevertheless *U-604* remained undetected, even with approaching corvettes sweeping the seas for enemy targets. This was one of the advantages of the small silhouette presented by the type VIIC. The conning tower was extremely difficult to spot in the darkness without the assistance of radar.

Höltring still exercised caution and steered at full speed in order to take up position immediately behind the sixth column of the convoy in an angle where the boat would remain almost invisible to the Allied lookouts. *U-604* moved to its new position, losing the approaching corvette in the process. Höltring ordered the two remaining torpedoes loaded so as to be able to mount one last attack on the convoy. He moved into a better firing position at high surfaced speed, his ambition being to attack the steamer trailing that column as soon as reloading was complete and before dawn made surfaced attack impossible. Unfortunately as *U-604* approached the target steamer the clouds parted and strong moonlight bathed *U-604* in light. The boat lay easily visible to escort ships and lookouts on nearby steamers in the left convoy column, and Höltring, deciding he could not wait for both torpedoes to be reloaded, attacked with the single one that was ready. As the convoy zigzagged back into the expected favourable firing position, *U-604* fired a single shot at 03.28 hours. Almost immediately *U-604* was spotted and came under artillery fire from the target steamer's defensive weapon. The first impact was a mere 30 metres from the German's conning tower and heralded other weapons opening fire on *U-604*. Immediately Höltring ordered a crash–dive and two further impacts were plainly heard aboard as *U-604* tilted into the depths. Meanwhile, after a seventy-five-second running time, the distinctive noise of a torpedo explosion was heard aboard the diving U-boat. This time-scale corresponded to an estimated distance of 1,125 metres. It was an ordinary-looking steamer with straight prow, single smokestack and loading crane by the bridge. From its situation in the water it was judged to be fully loaded. *U-604* had no time to dally and observe the results though, as it sank to a depth of 160 metres and began to attempt escape at slow creeping speed on electric motors.

Höltring steered a course of 100°, which would close the gap with the corvette and put the last attack to port of the U-boat. The boat was put on silent running and two Bold capsules were released in an attempt to fool enemy ASDIC. It wasn't long before the depth-charging began. At 03.37 hours six depth-charges were heard, though they were at some distance from the boat, possibly on the position of the Bolds. Over the next half an hour nine depth-charges were heard, the final explosion being at 04.07 hours, again far away. Thus the boat escaped its first real depth-charging, due to Höltring's correct appreciation of the dangerous situation he had been forced into. *U-604* would not always be so lucky in the future.

Above the escaping submarine, the torpedoed steamer had apparently merely been damaged by the attack and post-war records have failed to identify which ship it was. At about 06.08 hours *U-604* surfaced once more and prepared for a daylight attack. Once more the boat had to renew pursuit of the convoy which was sighted within the hour 20° on the starboard bow. However, further mechanical problems plagued the boat. After three quarters of an hour of continuous pursuit the boat's second compressor failed and could not be repaired with the tools available onboard. This meant that no new compressed air could be stored and thus that in the tanks was all that would be available for blowing tanks and surfacing the boat until *U-604* reached a friendly harbour.

After trailing SC 97 for about 200 nautical miles Höltring was faced with no other choice than to begin his return to port. His target was the French harbour of Brest on the Atlantic coast.

The remainder of the group designated Vorwärts – *U-609*, *U-92*, *U-756* and *U-91* – kept hounding the convoy. Kapitänleutnant Harney's *U-756* attempted an attack that same day, but it went disastrously wrong and the boat was sunk by HMCS *Morden* with all forty-three men on board killed.[18] Only *U-609* had managed to mount a successful attack on SC 97, sinking two ships on 31 August – the sole losses from the 59 ships of SC 97.

On the afternoon of 1 September *U-604* was forced to submerge rapidly to avoid air attack. While submerged, new attempts were made to repair the compressor but these too failed. Instead, in order to conserve the stored compressed air Höltring surfaced his boat dynamically, that is, by using the hydroplanes to steer the boat toward the surface. Once the hull had emerged he used the diesel engines' exhaust gases to blow the diving tanks clear. This also had the additional effect of preventing corrosion on the interior walls of the diving tanks due to the film of oil that remained from the exhaust gases. Though not an unusual procedure, it was far more complex than the customary surfacing using compressed air.

The following day a meeting of *U-604* and *U-609* was planned in order to pass spare parts for the compressors to Höltring, but it failed due to a bad weather front sweeping through the area. *U-604* continued its voyage without compressors and in steadily worsening weather, rated on the Beaufort scale as 7 to 8. If one considers that the scale runs from 0 to 12 one can obtain a good impression of the violence of the sea on this day. In plain language the weather was rated as near gale to gale force with waves between 4 and 5.5 metres high and the strain of the crew increased correspondingly. The bridge watch had to affix themselves to the conning tower with special webbing in order not to be washed overboard. The conning tower hatch needed to be closed despite travelling surfaced lest too much seawater be shipped inboard and swamp the U-boat. In general, however, the crew coped well, only a few men totally incapacitated with seasickness – though there was no shame in suffering the effects of such difficult conditions. U-boats had a characteristic reaction to high seas and that was to pitch and roll alarmingly, even in calmer waters. It had even happened that one U-boat had been forced to abort its patrol due to the seasickness of the entire crew, most of them too badly weakened by their state to be able to function with any degree of efficiency or safety.

As another example of the effect of seasickness on operational boats, Oberleutnant zur See Hans-Georg Hess aboard *U-995* had to deal with a radio operator severely afflicted. In order to at least keep the man able to work he hung an empty tin can around the man's neck into which he could vomit if necessary. Men who were badly affected could be considered by their commander a liability on future patrols. This happened to Hermann Friendrich aboard *U-96*. As an e-machinist he so badly suffered from seasickness during one war patrol that he vomited on the floor plating all around the electric motor room. Before the boat's next war patrol the captain hesitated as to whether he should take Friedrich again, only convinced by the man's promises that it would never happen again. Fortunately he was able to keep his promise and continue to serve aboard the famous *U-96*.[19]

Back at the scene of the hunting of SC 97, the remaining boats of the Vorwärts group were forced away by aircraft cover, regardless of the storm conditions. Catalinas of VP-73, USN, from Iceland arrived on the scene and *U-91* was slightly damaged by air attack. During the night of 2 September *U-91* attempted one unsuccessful shot before all boats broke off contact due to the increasing pressure from the Catalinas.[20]

Two days later the sea had moderated to strength 4 and *U-604* was able to rearrange its rendezvous with *U-609*. The spare parts for the compressor were packed into a waterproof container, a second empty container fastened to make it buoyant. Thus the spares were able to be transferred between the two boats. Apart from another crash-dive on 4 September to escape patrolling aircraft, the remainder of Höltring's voyage to Brest was relatively uneventful.

Naturally there were some minor errors from *U-604*'s crew during this their first patrol due to inexperience. One problem involved the operation of the boat's toilet while submerged. One member of the crew had neglected to close the pressure-balance valve after use with the result that he wore the contents of the toilet as he attempted to flush, as the outside water pressure was greater than the boat's internal pressure. Obviously this was unpleasant, but it could also be extremely dangerous: one boat was destroyed during the war when, against all rules, the sewage tanks were emptied with pressured air in broad daylight. Though submerged the U-boat's debris was spotted by an aeroplane which immediately dropped depth-charges. The boat suffered such severe damage that it had to be abandoned.

On 7 September a smoke cloud was sighted by *U-604*'s lookouts at 340°. Höltring assumed that it was an Allied ASW group and immediately began evasive manoeuvring. These ASW groups, also known as hunter-killer groups, had but one task: find and sink U-boats. Thus they had far more time available to search for and pursue any hostile contacts than would be available to a convoy escort, whose primary focus was protection, not offensive action. For this reason escorts had only limited time for U-boat hunts if contact was established and so their victory rate was relatively small at that stage of the war. Hunter-killer groups, however, were far more aggressive. The leading ship – the hunter – would probe with ASDIC for submerged U-boats. As soon as it had made contact, a second ship – the killer – would begin to attack the reported position with depth-charges. Any discovered U-boat had a vastly diminished chance of escape owing to this two-handed approach. If only a single ship was responsible for both ASDIC and depth-charging, then the opportunity to escape for the U-boat was much greater as the ship would take some time to reacquire the target after the disturbance of the water by the explosions and would need to manoeuvre into tracking position once more. This interruption in detection could be exploited by a competent U-boat skipper to make rapid course and depth changes and escape. Dividing the tasks between two attacking ships nearly eliminated this window of opportunity.

Höltring slipped away from the potential threat and during the next two days, while crossing Biscay, was forced to dive four more times by enemy aircraft. Biscay was becoming increasingly heavily patrolled by Allied aircraft as the transit points for U-boats to and from port. On 8 September *U-604* was immediately before Brest and rendezvoused with its escort into harbour, the armed trawler providing flak cover as it guided the U-boat through the defensive minefields. The crewmen not needed to run the boat were now able to gather on deck, many of whom had not tasted fresh air since departing Norway. It also allowed faster escape for those crewmen if *U-604* hit a mine. However, the boat was spared this fate and fastened to its pier in Brest at 20.50 hours. Naturally the customary reception committee was present, a band playing music and a curious crowd of onlookers and well-

Lehmann Willenbrock in his formal uniform.

wishers gathered dockside as the boat crept in quietly on electric motors. It was attached to the 9th U-Flotilla which had been commanded since 23 March 1942 by Heinrich Lehmann-Willenbrock who had sunk twenty-five ships totalling more than 180,000 BRT as captain of *U-96* in the course of eight war patrols.

Despite the enormous success which Lehmann-Willenbrock had achieved, he was still called the '*Oberbauernführer*' by many of his crews behind closed doors. This nickname came from his style of uniform, as he wore his trousers tucked into his boots and looked more like a farmer or *Obersturmbannführer* than a military officer. Coupled with this he was sometimes accompanied by the flotilla mascot – a goat that also sported a cape adorned with the emblem of the 9th U-Flotilla.

U-604 and its crew had completed their baptism of fire and could now leave behind the strain of the last few weeks. Certainly they had not escaped the effect of their time at sea. The majority of the crew had lost weight, though not because of the rations aboard the U-boat, as they were equipped with some of the best provisions in the Wehrmacht in order to maintain both physical and mental health. Nonetheless they celebrated with beer and songs upon their return:

'We're on our way to foaming beer, now that *U-604* has its arse on the pier!'

This time they had successfully returned to land without any problems. What would the next patrol bring?

Statement from BdU written in the War Diary for U-604 *covering the period from 4 August to 8 September 1942*

First operation for this commander aboard a new boat. It is unfortunate that good leadership and well executed attack on 1 September at about 00.45 hours yielded no success. No further remarks.

On its first war patrol *U-604* sank the *Abbekerk* on 25 August 1942; total tonnage 9,489 BRT. The sinking of the second ship from convoy SC 97 was not confirmed after the war.

During the period of *U-604*'s First War Patrol and the subsequent time spent in the shipyard before sailing again, the following U-boats were lost (4 August 1942 to 13 October 1942):

1	*U-372*	Neumann	sunk on	04.08.1942
2	*U-210*	Lemcke †	sunk on	06.08.1942
3	*U-379*	Kettner †	sunk on	08.08.1942
4	*U-578*	Rehwinkel †	sunk on	10.08.1942
5	*U-464*	Harms	sunk on	21.08.1942
6	*U-654*	Forstner †	sunk on	22.08.1942
7	*U-94*	Itcs	sunk on	28.08.1942
8	*U-756*	Harney †	sunk on	01.09.1942
9	*U-705*	Horn	sunk on	03.09.1942
10	*U-88*	Bohmann †	sunk on	12.09.1942
11	*U-589*	Horrer †	sunk on	14.09.1942
12	*U-261*	Lange †	sunk on	15.09.1942
13	*U-457*	Brandenburg †	sunk on	16.09.1942
14	*U-446*	Richard †	sunk on	21.09.1942
15	*U-253*	Friedrichs †	sunk on	25.09.1942
16	*U-165*	Hoffmann †	sunk on	27.09.1942
17	*U-162*	Wattenburg	sunk on	30.09.1942
18	*U-512*	Schultze †	sunk on	03.10.1942
19	*U-582*	Schulte †	sunk on	05.10.1942
20	*U-619*	Markowski	sunk on	05.10.1942
21	*U-179*	Sobe †	sunk on	08.10.1942
22	*U-171*	Pfeffer	sunk on	09.10.1942
23	*U-597*	Bopst †	sunk on	12.10.1942

†: Commander killed on board.

The Track Chart of the First War Patrol
   Days at sea for the first war patrol: 31
   Round trip distance: 5.955,2 nautical miles

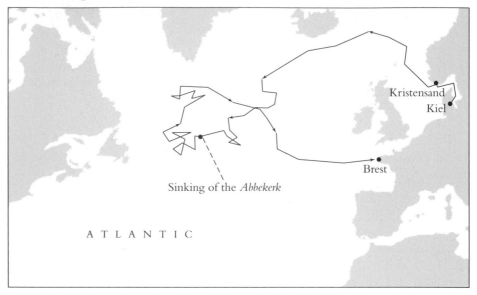

Kristensand

Kiel

Brest

Sinking of the *Abbekerk*

A T L A N T I C

Lehmann Willenbrock here seen as commander of *U-96* in his U-boat gear.

Above: Crewmen in Brest harbour. From left to right: Zentralemaat Robert Marquardt, Funkmaat Georg Seitz, Bootsmaat Peter Binnefeld, Torpedo Mechaniker Maat Ernst Schede and Maschinen Maat Fred Fröde. *Below*: Funkmaat Georg Seitz before *U-604*'s conning tower. The boat's flotilla emblem can be seen clearly on both the tower and Seitz's cap. *Right*: *U-604* in the newspaper.

Man muß sich zu helfen wissen.

5 m Turmhöhe ergibt 20 km Sicht bei 10 m Feindhöhe, 2 m Sehrohrhöhe ergibt 5 km Sicht bei 10 m
Feindhöhe, 7 m Höhe ergibt also 25 km Sicht bei
10 m Feindhöhe. Um den Sichtkreis des U-Bootes
zu erweitern, ließ der Kommandant das Sehrohr aus-
fahren, was den Blickpunkt des Beobachters um zwei
Meter erhöht. Was diese beiden Meter für eine
weitere Fernsicht bedeuten, zeigt die obige Rechnung.

Brest: the new home for U-604

One of France's oldest naval bases, Brest was taken over by the German Wehrmacht on 20 June 1940. It was ideally geographically situated for use as a U-boat base, the large French naval installation largely undamaged by the occupation. OKW soon designated it as one of the primary U-boat bases on the French Atlantic coast.

During 1941 as Allied air attacks became more frequent work began on a U-boat shelter. By mid-1942 it was operational.

Brest photographed while still a French naval port, the military base stretching from the harbour into the Penfeld River.

Brest U-boat bunker specifications:

Length:	306 m	
Width:	177 m	
Height:	18 m	
Surface area:	63,859 m²	
Roof thickness:	4 m	
Concrete required:	500,000 m³	
15 docks:	3 wet pens	112 m x 22m
	2 wet pens	93 m x 22 m
	8 dry docks	90 m x 15 m
	2 dry docks	103 m x 17 m

Brest was not the sole U-boat base on the French Atlantic coast. Lorient, St Nazaire, La Pallice and Bordeaux were also heavily used and all hosted further huge bunker complexes.

The bunker at Brest did not act as quarters for the men of the 9th U-Flotilla. Instead they occupied an unfinished hospital complex at Morvan. As it was located in the centre of the city a bus service was provided for the U-boat men. Physical separation at first proved beneficial as Allied air attacks were primarily directed against the harbour installations, not the city itself.

The headquarters of the 9th U-Flotilla in Brest.

Above: The U–Boat bunker in Brest seen from the air in September 1944. (With kind permission of the Bibliothek für Zeitgeschichte). *Below*: The large crane in Brest harbour basin.

The Second War Patrol

In the meantime, the technical war had gathered pace, the advantage initially held by the Allies. Since the middle of 1942 German U-boats had found themselves under increasing levels of air attack. The enemy seemed able to locate the submarines in both bad weather and at night with unerring accuracy. U-boat Command eventually and somewhat begrudgingly came to the conclusion that the aircraft must now be equipped with radar. In fact Allied aircraft were now becoming equipped with ASV (Mk 1) radar that operated on the 1.4 metre wavelength.[21]

In answer to this threat, German naval planners developed a radar warning device in conjunction with the French firm Metox, with which *U-604* was equipped before its second patrol. The Metox Model R 600 short-wave receiver generated an acoustic tone if it detected incoming radar pulses, thereby warning the U-boat crew. Thus the U-boat was given the ability to make an emergency dive in the event of enemy aircraft attack using radar. Officially the device was designated the FuMB 1 (*Funkmess-Beobachtungs-Gerät*), but the crews continued to refer to it simply as Metox.

However, the main initial drawback of the Metox was its antenna. Rushed into production and fitted as swiftly as possible to operational boats most in danger of enemy aircraft attack, there was no time to develop and install a proper waterproof mounting atop the conning tower. Thus the antenna comprised a simple wooden cross with the wire clamped to its edges. This was sufficient to detect incoming radar waves, but had to be rotated by hand on the conning tower and demounted every time the boat dived. The wire that connected the antenna to the receiver trailed through the open conning-tower hatch and so in the event of a crash-dive the wooden cross had to be thrown down on to the control room decking so that the hatch could be sealed. Needless to say they required constant repair. Nonetheless many boats were no doubt saved from enemy air attack and possible destruction by this somewhat rudimentary and makeshift device.[21]

Shortly after its introduction to service the Metox was given a new nickname by the French-based U-boat crews – the Biscay Cross, after the heavy air attacks in this area.

Before the Metox gear could be installed aboard *U-604* it had to be collected from an address in Boulevard Haussmann, Paris, which turned into something of an adventure for some of the crewmen. *U-604* became the first U-boat of the 9th U-Flotilla to be equipped with Metox. Funkmaat Georg Seitz later remembered the journey to retrieve the Metox gear:

Five men of our crew, including me, had the task of fetching a crate from an address in Paris. We didn't know anything at all about the contents, but if we had realised that bit was our flotilla's first Metox gear then we would not have gone about the whole business so carelessly. At the time, we travelled by train from Brest to Paris in order to find Boulevard Haussmann. At the address, which was a kind of naval branch office, we retrieved the crate without any problems. It was a relatively large wooden box which was fairly difficult to carry. We were able to drag the thing as far as the Metro, but once we were there we granted ourselves the luxury of hiring a porter. He was a black man who pushed the box on a small trolley about the station. And then it happened! We were briefly diverted and in an instant the porter was gone. We didn't know what had happened! How were we going to explain to the flotilla chief that the wooden box had been stolen by a railway porter? I didn't want to even think about the possible consequences. So we split up and everybody searched a sector of the Metro station. After minutes of desperate searching we found the porter exactly where he was supposed to be – waiting for us at the platform that our train would leave from. He had no intention at all of stealing from us!

So, what should we do in Paris with a radar receiver? Of course we still didn't even know that we had such a thing. Thus we became very relaxed and took the box finally on to the Metro. There we went to the North Paris Station from where we could go onwards to Brest. We would have been even more relaxed if only a few of our boys hadn't stolen some bananas from a fruit shop. We travelled by train with our stolen bananas. Once in Brest we were ordered to report to the flotilla chief Lehmann-Willenbrock. The bananas had not been a good idea as someone had identified us and we were sent before the commander to answer the charge. But he asked only if it had been any of us responsible, and we confessed. Following that he simply reprimanded us and then informed us that the matter was settled. We had, as it were, almost a free rein as the boat could hardly sail for its next patrol without us. But what would have happened if the porter really had stolen our crate? Nonetheless, we had successfully brought the first radar detector for our flotilla. I don't really want to think about what could have happened. They would probably have placed us before a court martial.

Indeed U-boat crewmen did have rather more free rein than other members of the Wehrmacht, not only on account of the peculiar nature of their service but also because Dönitz fiercely defended his men against any charges of mis-behaviour.

The evening before departing for their second patrol, the crew were obliged to pack all of their belongings – their estate, as it were. These were divided into service equipment and personal belongings and kept in a special room for the duration of the boat's patrol. The quarters occupied by the crew while ashore needed to be ready for other crews returning from sea. In the event that a boat was lost in action the personal belongings would be sent to their crewmen's next of kin. Nobody was better informed about the situation at the front and how grievous loses were becoming than the people assigned this onerous task.

U-604 sailed at 17.50 hours on 14 October 1942 from Brest on its second war patrol, the fifth of eleven boats that put to sea for operations in the South Atlantic. Of these eleven boats that sailed in October for war patrols, three were on their first operational voyages. The eleventh was a type XIV resupply U-boat heading for its operational region where it would serve to keep combat boats at sea for longer. None of the eleven would be lost on this patrol, though seven would be forced to break off their operations and return home prematurely.[22]

U-604 departed on electric motors from the safety of its dock within the expanse of the bunker. It proceeded along next to the harbour mole on which many onlookers, including the almost obligatory band and many women, had gathered to wish the crew a good voyage. Some bouquets of flowers were tossed on the boat's deck before it emerged from the harbour, through the narrow entrance channels and into the dangerous waters of Biscay toward the open Atlantic Ocean. It was the first operational voyage that had the same departure and return point for *U-604* and this marked an important distinction: the object of the voyage was not to reach a distant port, but to search for merchant ships and sink them. The new operational zone of the South Atlantic was welcomed by the crew, as they considered the balmy waters would make life more comfortable aboard ship.

During the course of the war the navigable waters before the occupied harbours were repeatedly mined by Allied aircraft and *U-604* travelled the first few nautical miles in the wake of an escort ship that not only guided the U-boat

An Enigma code machine. (With kind permission of Bibliothek für Zeitgeschichte)

through the defensive minefields but also protected it from possible unknown enemy ones. This escort consisted of a Sperrbrecher, a large converted freighter whose holds had been filled with buoyant material. It also emitted a strong magnetic field from an electrical coil aboard that would activate magnetic mines within range of the ship.[23] Should the Sperrbrecher hit a contact mine, the buoyant material would keep it afloat. Nonetheless all but a skeleton crew were ordered to remain on the deck of *U-604* in life jackets until the potential and existing minefields were cleared.

At 23.05 hours *U-604* left its escort and began the voyage into the increasingly perilous Bay of Biscay on its own. During the following two days the boat sailed surfaced only at night so as to offer enemy pilots no target during daylight hours. After three uneventful days the listening gear detected a corvette, a crash-dive saving the boat from detection. Once submerged an unknown sound signature was clearly audible which led the Germans crew to believe that the Allies had employed a new underwater detection system. Nonetheless, Höltring ordered the boat surfaced after two hours. During the next four uneventful days *U-604* covered 681 nautical miles, with only daily test dives and a single crash-dive to break the monotony. On 22 October a neutral ship was sighted which could not be attacked; its identity was clear from the white superstructure and coloured smokestack. Neutral ships were generally brightly coloured and travelled lit at night, as opposed to the darkened grey hulls of the protagonist countries.

U-604 was directed first to operate with the Streitaxt group that BdU had gathered on 23 October to hunt for a convoy reported by Beobachtungsdienst, the German cryptanalytical department. From 1942, British Admiralty radio traffic had been decoded and read by German listening stations giving Dönitz a reasonably clear picture of where the convoys were likely to travel and allowing him to plan his boats' dispositions accordingly. What he did not know was that the Allies had penetrated his 'Triton' Enigma code with which he communicated with his boats.[24] The Allies had captured an intact Enigma machine from *U-110* and were able to read German signal traffic and thus reroute convoys away from gathering U-boat groups, all directed by radio communication from BdU. Dönitz, although suspicious that the British knew his intentions, refused to accept that the Enigma could have been compromised and continued to believe that the British source of intelligence was from elsewhere.

This group, Streitaxt, which BdU had gathered in the presumed path of the convoy comprised the following U-boats: *U-131* (Schendel), *U-203* (Kottmann), *U-409* (Massmann), *U-509* (Witte), *U-510* (Neitzel), *U-572* (Hirsacker), *U-604* (Höltring) and *U-659* (Stock).[25] Of these, *U-203* had a particularly remarkable recent history. Before ObltzS Hermann Kottmann had taken command of the boat, Kaptäleutnant Rolf Mützelburg had been captain. An 'Ace' commander, he had been awarded the Oak Leaves to his Knight's Cross before his untimely death. While on patrol in the Atlantic during September he had indulged in a swimming break with members of his crew, during which he dived from the top of the boat's conning tower. Unfortunately the boat rolled slightly in the gentle swell and he struck the saddle tank with his head and died some time later from the severe head injury sustained.[26] His death in such a 'banal' fashion was virtually disguised in reporting by the U-boat leadership lest it harm the myth of the Sea Wolves.

From 23 October *U-604* continued its journey toward the allocated operational area. The following evening at 19.48 hours aerial bombs were heard exploding in the distance. Höltring immediately dived and commenced an underwater search through his boat's hydrophones, detecting eighteen explosions during the next hour. The distant sound of screw noises was also detected though they receded and Höltring surfaced to continue his voyage.

Convoy SL 125 was found by *U-203* on 25 October. It comprised forty-two ships sailing from Freetown to Liverpool, primarily carrying troops returning to the United Kingdom. The escort for this convoy was minimal despite the presence of troop transport, only four corvettes shepherding the merchant ships.[27] *U-604* received the order to make for grid-square DH 8444 and lie in wait. While en route, the distant sound of twenty-eight depth-charges echoed through the water but *U-604* pressed on and reached its operational area, one day later the shout from the bridge that everybody waited for: 'Mastheads in sight!'

However, Höltring had found not the convoy but a solo sailing ship. None-theless with little chance of depth-charge retaliation he decided to attack. The mastheads that had been sighted at 09.36 hours turned out to be the first signs of a tanker which was steering 60° at 12 knots. After scarcely a quarter of an hour the lookouts on the bridge also sighted another U-boat at an approximate distance of 4 miles.

After twenty minutes *U-604* dived to prepare an underwater attack on the tanker which was steering directly for the boat. It was not often that a target sailed directly in front of a U-boat's torpedo tubes. But to Höltring's regret, this situation did not last long. The tanker zigzagged so much that the U-boat never came near to its intended target. Undeterred, Höltring prepared a three-shot spread at 12.24 hours on what was now a target 3,500 metres away. Almost predictably, all torpedoes missed by a long way.

In the meantime the grey-painted tanker continued to alter course and had come close enough for the 15.2 cm cannon on its deck to be clearly recognised. Although there was no national flag on the stern, there were several smaller calibre weapons to be seen on the bridge and bow. But nothing altered the fact that Höltring had missed.

After another hour *U-604* surfaced and continued the chase, using its superior surfaced speed to pass the tanker and begin another attack. While the U-boat raced ahead all tubes were reloaded. The zigzags that were completed by the tanker at 16.00 hours were so pronounced that Höltring assumed that she must be attempting to avoid another U-boat, Höltring well aware that there were other German boats operating in the area. These manoeuvres were not the only diffi-culty in pursuing that tanker, as the weather was also deteriorating. Shortly after-wards, lookouts lost sight of their quarry as it disappeared into a rain shower but by 19.15 hours Höltring was in his planned attack position, lying in wait where he believed the general course steered by the tanker would be. Half an hour later the distant U-boat was briefly sighted once more before the tanker hove into view.

At 20.05 hours Höltring dived to begin his attack and this time he had better luck than before. The tanker passed within 500 metres of *U-604* and at 21.06 hours a single shot from the stern tube was fired. At that range it was a simple shot and within half a minute the sound of detonation echoed through the water.

The *Anglo Maersk*, sunk on 27 October 1942 by *U-604* west of the Canary Islands.

But the tanker refused to sink. After twenty minutes of observation Höltring surfaced to deliver a *coup-de-grâce* on the stationary ship. There was the chance that the damaged tanker could remain afloat and be towed by the Allies to the Canary Islands and repaired. But after the first finishing shot, the situation remained unchanged, the tanker wallowing slightly deeper in the swell, but remaining stable. Höltring ordered a second shot to finish the ship which struck the tanker at 22.18 hours. Two minutes later violent explosions erupted from the tanker, so much so that the men on *U-604* had the impression they were under attack. In order to avoid this presumed bombardment Höltring submerged for half an hour and four minutes after he resurfaced the crippled tanker sank.

The British motor tanker carried the name *Anglo Maersk* and had been built by the firm W. G. Armstrong, Whitworth & Co. Ltd in Newcastle upon Tyne in 1930. Originally the ship had been designated *Anglo Swede*, but had had its name changed in 1932. Eight years later it was taken over from its owner, the London firm Houlder Brothers & Co., by the British War Transport commission and placed into Admiralty service. Attached to convoy SL 125 she was travelling in ballast bound for Glasgow, having left Freetown on 16 October, when Höltring had found the ship separated from the rest of SL 125.

The tanker had become detached because *U-604* was not the first U-boat to have torpedoed her. *U-509* had attacked the ship on 26 October and hit her, damaging some machinery. MV *Anglo Maersk* was straggling from the rest of the convoy unable to keep pace with them. The entire crew of captain, thirty-two sailors and two gunners was able to escape the ship in lifeboats before she went down and reached the island of Hierro in the Canaries two days later. They were fortunate that the tanker was travelling in ballast and not loaded with its usual cargo when hit. It was almost considered suicidal for sailors to serve aboard tankers or munitions ships. Not only were tankers primary targets for attacking U-boats but there was little chance of escape if hit. If a tanker was torpedoed and crewmen did manage to abandon ship they were often trapped in pools of burning liquid. In turn if the fuel did not burn, the oil burnt the fragile membranes of survivors' lungs as they often inadvertently inhaled the spilt oil and seawater if swimming to safety. Likewise munitions ships were favoured targets and if hit often exploded with such violence that not only were the crew doomed, but the attacking U-boats frequently damaged.

After the sinking of the tanker *U-604* continued to operate against SL 125 which was by now south-west of the Canaries and headed north. Already 90 per cent of Streitaxt had converged on the convoy. That same day Werner Witte in

The British corvette HMS *Petunia*. (With kind permission of Bibliothek für Zeitgeschichte)

U-509 sank two British ships: the *Pacific Star* and *Stentor*.[28] But unfortunately for Höltring, on 28 October two British escort corvettes, one of them probably HMS *Petunia*, sighted *U-604*.

Höltring managed to outmanoeuvre this pair of escorts who possessed little time for extended ASW hunts. *U-604* dived around 21.41 hours to use the underwater listening gear, its capabilities far superior to visual search. The range of the boat's listening gear – *Horchanlage*, designated *GHG* for *Gruppenhorchanlage* – was impressive. Single sailing ships could be detected at 20 kilometres, convoys at up to a hundred. This far exceeded the abilities of bridge lookouts that could not see that far even under perfect conditions due to the Earth's curvature. Thus the frequent use of submerged sound searches became a popular tactic among U-boat commanders.

Through the headphones two explosions were heard at 69°, possibly from another pair of ships torpedoed by Witte. One was the 5,178-ton *Hopecastle*, the other the 5,283-ton *Nagpore*. Shortly after this four depth-charges were heard. Höltring surfaced to resume the chase, but *U-604* was forced away on 29 October at 03.32 hours by what Höltring believed was an enemy destroyer. But Höltring returned doggedly to the convoy trail and set course 130° to head them off. By 11.20 hours he had reached his desired position and dived where his listening gear detected the sound of multiple screws approaching. *U-604* lay at a depth of only 20 metres as an escort ship sailed overhead, unaware of their presence. Höltring dived deeper and waited for the convoy to come within range. Scarcely an hour later he was back at periscope depth. At about 18.30 hours despite heavy weather and a sea state of 6 to 7, a single tanker was sighted. Höltring immediately began his attack, but an escort also came into view and his plans were foiled as the ships disappeared within two hours into a rain shower. He ordered another sweep with the listening gear, but failed to detect the ships. *U-604* surfaced and continued the hunt on diesel engines.

Shortly after midnight on 30 October, four torpedo detonations were heard, later attributed to the sinking of the following ships: the *Brittany* sunk by *U-509* and the freighter *Bullmouth*, torpedoed by *U-409* Massmann.[29] *U-604* passed one of the sinking ships and Höltring knew that the convoy could not be far away. At 04.06 hours the lookouts shouted: 'Shadow in sight!'

However, it took another two hours to identify the shadow as part of the hunted convoy. *U-604* tracked the mastheads that had become visible and orientated itself with the convoy track. Höltring wanted to wait for dawn before attacking again whereupon he began his attack against a steamer. Höltring had already found an advantageous firing position against the large steamer and, shortly after firing, two explosions were clearly heard. Höltring believed that he had hit a passenger ship of 11,000 BRT, perhaps one of the prized troop transports. The steamer immediately went up in flames, and several individual explosions were heard as flares rose in all direction from the blaze. But this demonstration could not be observed for long as the point ship of the port column began an artillery bombardment against *U-604*. Höltring dived to escape at 21.24 hours and after six minutes two more explosions were heard followed by clear sinking noises – the death throes of their target. In fact it was the 1,898-ton MV *President Doumer* that had been sunk. Built in 1934 by Societé Provençale de Constructions Navales, it belonged to the Bibby Line in Liverpool, its home port Aden. It acted as troop transport in SL 125 and carried 260 passengers on board. After the torpedo hit, panic had erupted on board so that most life rafts were not launched correctly and wrecked. Many jumped into the sea to escape the sinking ship, seventy-eight crewmen and seven gunners rescued by the steamer *Alaska* and HMS *Cowslip* from the convoy, while 260 were lost, including the master.

Tragically, two hours after having rescued the survivors of the *President Doumer*, the *Alaska* was also torpedoed, this time by *U-510*. Again, panic broke out aboard the ship and part of the crew abandoned her into life rafts. However, this time the ship was not sunk and managed to limp into neutral Lisbon, arriving there on 11 November. In the forty-five minutes since Höltring's successful attack, five further torpedo explosions were heard in the submerged *U-604*, the result of damage inflicted on the 6,405 BRT *Tasmania*, by Kapitänleutnant Stock aboard *U-659*.[30] At around 22.36 hours Höltring brought his boat back to the surface to again pursue SL 125.

Since he had been running submerged at low speed he once again had to make a significant surfaced dash on main engines to find another shooting position. At 23.02 hours three sinking ships were seen by the lookouts, until finally an intact steamer was also sighted. Höltring did not hesitate: he fired a torpedo which hit the ship and immediately put the stern underwater. However, there was little time to observe the effect of his shooting as another target sailed into view. This too was at close range, passing the burning hulks and Höltring fired another torpedo at the new ship at 23.19 hours. This time there was no corresponding explosion. According to later statements by Chief Engineer Jürgens and the hydrophone operator it was a perfect shot and the metallic impact of the torpedo could be clearly heard after a running time of fifty-two seconds. Thus the impact pistol on the torpedo must have malfunctioned, although it is possible that it was also a ricochet. If a torpedo impacted at too acute an angle there was not enough impact to trigger the pistol and bring about detonation: the torpedo would scrape off the hull and miss.

The *President Doumer* sunk on 30 October 1942 by *U-604*.

Within ten minutes Höltring tried again, but this time it was a clear miss as the steamer turned after the torpedo had been fired. Now all four bow tubes had been fired and Höltring was left with only the stern tube. He therefore decided to await a more certain opportunity rather than waste his final shot.

The second ship that *U-604* had sunk that night was the British SS *Baron Vernon*, with a tonnage of 3,642 tons. It had been built by D. & W. Henderson & Co. Ltd of Glasgow in 1932, and was carrying 5,500 tons of iron ore when sunk. Like the tanker *Anglo Maersk*, this freighter had sailed from Freetown on 16 October, torpedoed two weeks later. All forty-nine crew members were saved by *Baron Elgin* from SL 125 and later landed in Madeira.

Once again Höltring operated on the presumed course of SL 125. Heinz Hirsacker's *U-572* was sighted that day. Hirsacker would suffer a tragic fate in 1943 when he was executed for supposed cowardice in the face of the enemy, the only case of this within the U-boat service.

At about 17.42 hours on 31 October *U-604* was again forced away by enemy escorts, and an hour after that had to make an emergency dive to avoid aircraft attack. Once the danger had passed *U-604* surfaced again and resumed the chase, although once more the audible chirps from the Metox heralded yet another aircraft approaching. This pattern began to repeat over and over again and on the morning of 1 November Dönitz called off the pursuit of SL 125 due to the intensifying aircraft threat. Previously, such heavy air cover by RAF Coastal

A depth–charge launcher aboard an Allied escort ship.
(With kind permission of Bibliothek für Zeitgeschichte)

Command had led to substantial losses to the U-boats against other convoys. *U-604* began its return voyage. The Streitaxt Group had been led into the area west of Gibraltar by the pursuit and *U-604* was still in the vicinity of *U-203* and *U-409* who were also returning due to lack of fuel. The damaged *U-659* likewise began its homebound journey to France.

The battle with SL 125 had taken eight days and seven of the ten U-boats of the Streitaxt Group had managed to sink twelve Allied ships totalling 80,505 tons with no loss to themselves. Additionally the 5,681-ton Alaska had been damaged by *U-510*.[31] The human loss to the convoy had been substantial, although tactically the loss to the Allies actually transpired to be relatively minor. SL 125 had ironically – and tragically – been a valuable distraction of U-boat force away from other Allied convoys bound for the Operation Torch landings which were imminent on the coast of Morocco. Besides, the Allies were aware of the concentration of U-boats that had gathered to oppose SL 125 and the greater need of the invasion force apparently prevailed.

On the morning of 1 November at 08.23 hours *U-604* dived to avoid aircraft and detected the noise of steamer screws mixed with the higher pitch of a destroyer. At periscope depth Höltring observed a stationary destroyer at a kilometre distance. The unfavourable angle rendered attack impossible and not long afterward the fingers of ASDIC closed around *U-604*. Höltring dived to 150 metres and for the first time *U-604* came under direct depth-charge attack.

Now, as the U-boat crew would say, it became psychological. A hunt with depth-charges strained the crew's nerves; the U-boat, completely outclassed, sped by the surface hunter, reliant on the commander's changes of depth and direction to avoid location and destruction. The sole contact with the enemy lay through the sound man and his listening gear. He in turn painted an overview for the commander. In order to reduce the stress on the crew, Höltring and his radio man used certain procedures, one of which was not to refer to the destroyer as such but by the seemingly harmless acronym 'vehicle'. If the sound man cried 'Vehicle approaching', the entire crew were aware that the enemy destroyer had found them and was preparing to drop depth-charges on their position. Höltring could then choose: left or right? Naturally the enemy captain was also aware of those choices, and so the cat-and-mouse game continued. Only coincidence and luck could determine whether the U-boat steered into or away from danger.

Also, the commander had to be aware of the psychological effect that his demeanour had on the crew. If he appeared nervous or uncertain the crew would feel their lives in acute danger. In this case, the enemy destroyer passed directly overhead twice and each time dropped seven depth-charges on *U-604*. These exploded around the boat at 130 and 110 metres. Bulbs aboard *U-604* shattered under the concussion, otherwise there was complete silence. Another surface warship soon arrived to assist in the hunt and they began to use the 'hunter-killer' tactic against *U-604*.

Höltring now faced the additional danger of having to conserve his battery power under what could be an extended hunt. This was a prime vulnerability for World War II U-boats. If a captain used high speed on his electric motors, the batteries would soon be depleted, in which case the boat would be unable to maintain its depth and be faced with two choices: surface or sink forever into the depths. Such a situation generally resulted in the sinking of the U-boat as it was forced to surface under the waiting guns of the Allied hunters above. The U-boat's surface armament was inconsequential compared with that of a destroyer or corvette and, besides, a U-boat was more vulnerable to damage from gunfire. However, Höltring kept his nerve and kept his boat at slow manoeuvring speed, to minimise the risk of battery exhaustion as far as possible.

It was some time before he was able to shake free of his pursuers, twenty-three depth-charges having been dropped around *U-604* before Höltring managed to

Above: Commandant Horst Höltring greets the welcoming party on the pier. *Below*: *U-604* has already tied up, *U-659* approaches the pier. *Below left*: An article from the period that shows *U-604* at the pier in the foreground, *U-659* behind. *Below right*: The Flotilla Chief of the 9th U-Flotilla, Lehmann Willenbrock, welcomes *U-604*. Trailing from the periscope can be seen the three sinking pennants signifying *U-604*'s successes.

Above: Part of the crew in Brest harbour. In the background is the entrance to the military harbour. *Below*: *U-604* enters Brest.

Below: U-604 has already tied up. *Below:* Lehmann Willenbrock greets Commander Höltring.

Above: On the right, *U-604*, left *U-659*, while in the background *U-409* is entering harbour. *Below*: The three U-boat commanders, from left to right: *U-659*, Stock, *U-409*, Massmann and *U-604*, Höltring. Commandant Stock lost his life seven months later in the Atlantic when *U-659* was rammed by *U-439* (von Tippelskirch); *U-659* sank within seconds and only three men from the bridge watch were saved, forty-four others going to the deep. *U-439* also sank, only nine of its crew surviving. It was the worst such collision suffered by the U-boat service during World War II. Nine months after this photograph was taken Massmann was sunk in the Mediterranean aboard *U-409*. He survived.

Above: Welcoming the crew home. *Below*: The incoming boats in a group on the harbour.

slip free. *U-604* was virtually unharmed, only the flooding controls had been damaged. The crew breathed a collective sigh of relief – they had survived their first depth-charge hunt. Life returned normal for the boat when it surfaced after four hours below the waves. But, of course, they could not remain there, and they were forced to make a crash-dive at 21.48 hours to avoid aircraft, which had not been picked up by Metox but rather heard by the bridge watch despite the noise of the diesels. After this lucky escape the remainder of their return voyage was uneventful and *U-604* together with *U-659* and *U-409* rendezvoused with their escort near Brest at 11.10 hours on 5 November.

As had become customary among U-boat crews, a white pennant was made to signify each ship sunk – red for warships. These were made from bed sheets and the tonnage of the victim painted on. *U-604* trailed three such pennants from its extended periscope as it ran into Brest harbour. At around 14.00 hours all three boats were tied to the dock in front of the U-boat shelters and the mandatory welcoming ceremonies began. Naturally, even some women managed to come aboard and welcome the crew with what a contemporary witness described as 'kisses left and right!'. The crew were awarded the coveted U-boat badge at the end of this trip, signifying two patrols at sea. Only in exceptional circumstances was it awarded after only one patrol.

The 1 WO, Wolfgang Poeschel, left *U-604* after this trip and was transferred to the U-boat commander's school in order to receive his own boat. Later as commander of *U-422* he would make a single patrol beginning on 1 August 1943. The boat was sunk with all hands north of the Azores without a single success.

During October 1942 the majority of German U-boats continued to operate in the North Atlantic and doing the month sank 89 ships with a tonnage of 583,690 BRT, the following month these figures swelling to 126 ships totalling 802,160 BRT.[32]

Statement from BdU written in the War Diary for U-604 *covering the period from 9 September to 5 November 1942*

For the duration of the undertaking, the success is pleasing.

In detail, note the following point:

Concerning the single sailing tanker, shooting at an estimated distance of 3,500 m was unnecessary. Better to remain doggedly aiming at the target and attempt to achieve a more favourable firing position.

Against the convoy on 30 October, after contact at around 08.59 hours the attack should have been launched in daylight. Considering the relatively weak convoy protection, the boat could have probably attacked again at night.

When regaining the convoy, and also when losing it, radio communication merely stated: 'Convoy in sight' and/or 'lost'. It is imperative that an indication of the location, course and speed is communicated as well . . .

Track Chart For The Second War Patrol
Sea days for the second war patrol: 24
Round trip: 3,810 nautical miles

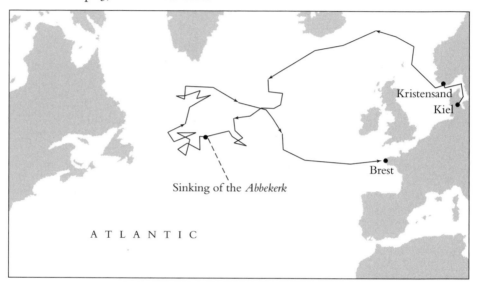

Sinking of the *Abbekerk*

ATLANTIC

During the Second War Patrol *U-604* sank the following ships: the tanker estimated at 9,000 BRT sunk on 27 October was *Anglo Maersk* (7,705 BRT). *Baron Vernon* (3.642 BRT) and *President Doumer* (11.889 BRT) were both sunk on 30 October 1942, total tonnage, 23.236 BRT.

In the period of *U-604*'s second war patrol and time spent under repair in the shipyard before the third patrol the following U-boats were sunk by the Allies. (14 October to 25 November 1942).

1	*U-661*	Lilienfeld †	sunk on	15.10.1942
2	*U-353*	Römer	sunk on	16.10.1942
3	*U-216*	Schultz †	sunk on	20.10.1942
4	*U-412*	Jahrmärker †	sunk on	22.10.1942
5	*U-599*	Breizhaupt †	sunk on	24.10.1942
6	*U-627*	Kindelbacher †	sunk on	27.10.1942

7	*U-520*	Schwartkopf †	sunk on	30.10.1942
8	*U-559*	Heidtman	sunk on	30.10.1942
9	*U-658*	Senkel †	sunk on	30.10.1942
10	*U-132*	Vogelsangl †	sunk on	05.11.1942
11	*U-408*	Hymmen †	sunk on	05.11.1942
12	*U-658*	Senkel †	sunk on	30.10.1942
13	*U-660*	Baur	sunk on	12.11.1942
14	*U-411*	Spindlegger †	sunk on	13.11.1942
15	*U-605*	Schütze †	sunk on	14.11.1942
16	*U-595*	Faslam	sunk on	14.11.1942
17	*U-259*	Köpke†	sunk on	15.11.1942
18	*U-98*	Eichmann †	sunk on	15.11.1942
19	*U-173*	Schweichel †	sunk on	16.11.1942
20	*U-331*	Thiesenhausen	sunk on	17.11.1942
21	*U-184*	Dangschat †	sunk on	20.11.1942

†: Commander killed on board.

U-boat Recreation Centre at Trevarez, Chateauneuf de Fou

Once again the crew had survived their war patrol. Within a day of returning to Brest the entire crew were sent to rest and recuperate in the U-boat recreation centre established in the red brick Chateau Trevarez (erroneously called the 'Castle Chateauneuf' by the Germans). In the jargon of the U-boat crews, the centre was known as the 'U-Boat Pastures'. This particular centre was located in the chateau near the picturesque town of Chateauneuf de Fou deep within Brittany's countryside.

The 'Red Castle' – Chateau Trevarez..

Part of the crew of *U-604* outside the Chateau Trevarez.

Officially the crew were allocated ten days of peace and quiet in wonderful surrounding countryside with sports and cultural activities. The truth was a little different. An interview with one of *U-604*'s crew shows other pleasures to be high on the list of activities:

In the castle were the female personnel who had served the previous owner and they actively welcomed us U-boat men. The kitchen was excellent and the cellar full of champagne and the best French wine. Oh, and the best thing was: we had unrestricted use of everything!

The Third War Patrol

Although the U-boat men at that time did not know it, statistically the next war patrol that *U-604* sailed on should have been their last one. Statisticians within the U-boat arm computed that the majority of U-boats were sunk on their third patrol. For obvious reasons, statistics of this kind were not revealed to the German public or even discussed among members of the Wehrmacht. Even after the war the figures only really came to light after the interrogation of Admiral Eberhard Godt (2nd Unterseebootsführungsabteilung) by his British captors. He was asked why the training of the U-boat crews between patrols diminished as the war progressed. The provision of improved equipment aboard the boats would have demanded this. The answer he provided was that the life expectancy of a U-boat was three patrols. Therefore the extended training of crews was not necessary.[33]

Of course, the crew of *U-604* knew nothing of these numbers, and even if they had nothing would have changed. The boat still had to sail. After three weeks in the Brest shipyard, *U-604* slipped from harbour at 16.21 hours on 26 November as the thirty-eighth boat of forty-four that sailed for the North Atlantic that month. Among them were three re-supply U-boats and fourteen that were on their first patrols. Five boats would be lost, three from those on their maiden operational voyage. Four more would be forced to abort their patrols due to damage.[34]

During November 1942 Axis submarines would sink 126 ships totalling 802,160 tons. During the following month this number dropped to 64 ships totalling 337,618 tons.[35]

At 22.17 hours *U-604* left its escort and headed west. Within twelve minutes the Metox emitted its audible alarm and the boat made its first crash-dive. *U-604* sailed submerged for forty-one minutes before surfacing once more only to be driven almost straight back under. This pattern repeated itself twice more that night as the Allies deployed their new weapon in the ASW arsenal – the Leigh Light.

The Leigh Light was an oversized searchlight with a diameter of 61 centimetres.

One was installed beneath the bearing edge of a bomber, angled so that it could cast its light to a range of 5,000 metres. If a U-boat was located by radar in the night, Allied bomber crews were now able to attack them effectively.[36] Naturally the searchlight was not switched on until the last moment, often giving the impression of appearing from nowhere and blinding the unsuspecting U-boat lookouts. Furthermore, the Allies were aware of Metox and tended only to switch their radar on periodically so as to reduce the chance of warning potential target U-boats.

Naturally there were teething troubles with the new weapon and some aircraft were lost, but these issues were solved with harsh experience and the result was substantially in the Allies favour; the shelter of darkness denied to surfaced U-boats as the life of the U-boat crews grew ever more dangerous.

On the morning of the second day *U-604* continued its voyage submerged. A single contact was made on listening gear and Höltring surfaced to attempt to locate the distant ship, but it eluded them. While sailing submerged the U-boats were unable to receive radio traffic and this gave BdU a problem: they needed a precise overview of the vessels' locations in order to exercise tight control over the boats at sea. This was to enable them to plan the formation of mobile hunting groups based on the very latest intelligence. For this reason, BdU allocated a number to each message transmitted, so that when they surfaced the radio men could check that all the transmissions had been received and a complete picture could be formed. If a U-boat kept submerging one of the messages could be missed, but the radio operator would know and could ask for that particular transmission to be sent again.

This was why *U-604* received the following transmission:

FT Incoming. Repetition of 27.11.1942 for Höltring. Contents of guidance number 15: All boats. Immediately prohibition is lifted in Grid Square BE, attack convoy. England-Gibraltar traffic with war material in this sea-area is expected. From there: Charge, attack, and at the same time report contacts . . . Hang on . . .

It may seem strange that permission to attack was required to be expressly given, but the reasoning behind this is as follows: If a U-boat sighted enemy convoy traffic it was not allowed to attack immediately but rather was required to hold the contact and transmit regular signals giving the convoy's position, course and speed so that other U-boats could be gathered. Once they had, BdU slipped lose its tight rein on the boats and let them attack.

During the following night, at 01.07 hours, *U-604* was forced to dive again because of radar detection by the Metox. Höltring elected to surface as he reasoned that they would likely be undisturbed. Fortunately he was proved correct and *U-604* sailed undisturbed until daybreak where she dived once more to proceed submerged. At around midday three detonations were heard. Since there were no Allied aircraft stationed nearby, the explosions were assumed to have originated from escorting aircraft and Höltring stayed submerged. As night closed in the boat surfaced once more at 18.55 hours to continue surfaced and allow the batteries to be charged. The following night passed without incident and once more *U-604* dived with the sunrise.

Beginning at midday again, some eighteen explosions were heard, all presumed to be depth-charges. Two hours later Höltring surfaced and steered west into the Atlantic. That night a light cruiser was spotted at a distance of seven nautical miles, emerging from a rain cloud. With an estimated speed of 20 knots there was no chance of pursuit and Höltring continued to cruise toward his area of operations. The entry in *U-604*'s radio log on 1 December 1942 at 15.12 hours was:

1 Group 'Draufgänger' from 5 December 20.00 hours in sequence 'Höltring' . . . Patrol line from . . . to . . . Convoy expected to be headed southwest from 6 December.
2 'Hinsch' and 'Höltring' to turn at 20.00 hours . . . America 1. Boats belong to the group 'Draufgänger'.

Thus the boat was integrated into the Draufgänger hunting group, waiting as part of its patrol line for the expected convoy traffic. The term 'America 1' used in the second transmission denoted a change over in radio frequencies to this so-named channel. The Atlantic was divided operationally into different frequencies so that the wireless crews aboard the various located boats could concentrate solely on traffic meant for their region.

The following day brought the weak sound of more distant screw noises as *U-604* sailed onwards until, on 2 December as the boat sailed approximately 2,000km west of Calais in the Atlantic, *U-604* sighted its goal. At 12.31 hours a steamer hove into view at 342°, Höltring immediately altering course to bring the target into a firing position. However, the ship had a high surface speed, estimated by the lookouts to be 17.4 knots and Höltring was constantly frustrated by the target's erratic zigzagging as it outpaced pursuit. A dilemma faced the young captain as he ordered the boat to continue the chase at full surfaced speed to close the distance, attempting to use the electric motors to provide some additional drive for the propellers. The target continued its zigzagging and Höltring was constantly frustrated in his attempts to attain a decent firing position. But at least

U-604 had not been spotted. At about 18.30 hours the Germans' fortunes changed as the ship made a general course alteration to the south, now steering into an advantageous position for Höltring to attack. Also, the target was now steering into a high swell resulting in a loss of 1 to 1.5 knots speed as well.

Höltring was forced to switch off his motors due to rapidly dwindling charge, but by this stage *U-604* was halfway toward a more optimal firing position, the target ship running independently into the U-boat's path. Höltring continued surfaced as he felt the small silhouette of the U-boat would be unlikely to be seen from the steamer.

Around 19.35 hours the ship lay directly before the U-boat, with a speed of 16 knots, zigzagging again after ten minutes. Höltring planned a bow torpedo attack at 20.07 hours. However, the ship veered sharply away as part of its erratic path and Höltring was unable to attack with his planned bow salvo. Instead he was forced to make a single shot from the boat's loaded stern tube, which he did at 20.15 hours. The ship lay 800 metres from the U-boat and Höltring's aim was true. The torpedo impacted and exploded and within three minutes the ship began to sink, gone within another two minutes bow first into the depths.

He recorded his target as a single-stack passenger steamer with sloping prow. For armament the ship presumably carried a disguised gun platform at the stern. Höltring recorded that he had just sunk a ship resembling the American 'Brazil' type, estimated at 12,000 BRT.

A life raft was sighted with three survivors clinging to it, and *U-604* approached in order to verify the name of the destroyed ship. The bridge watch managed to glean from the trio that the target had been 16,000 BRT, as noted by Höltring after hearing from the men on the aft that the ship's name was '*Ceomi*' (They had mispronounced it.)

At 20.50 hours *U-604* continued at half-speed on course 353°, charging the batteries as the boat travelled, and leaving the shipwrecked survivors behind. *U-604* was, like every U-boat, unable to rescue survivors of sinking ships under new standing orders from BdU. The German U-boats had received firm instructions that no shipwrecked survivors were to be rescued as U-boats engaged in this action had been attacked in the past. The final act that had led to this decision had been the so-called 'Laconia Affair' after which Dönitz issued the following order by radio on 17 September 1942:[37]

1 No attempt of any kind must be made at rescuing members of ships sunk, and this includes picking up persons from the water and placing them in lifeboats, righting capsized lifeboats and issuing food and water. Rescue runs counter to the rudimentary demands of warfare for the destruction of

enemy ships and crews.

2 Orders for bringing back captains and chief engineers still apply.

3 Rescue the shipwrecked only if their statements would be of benefit to your boat.

4 Be harsh, bear in mind that the enemy takes no regard of women and children in his bombing attacks on German cities.

Nonetheless many U-boat commanders continued to supply lifeboats with provisions and charts, but the time of Prize Rules was long over. This honour code prescribed in World War I had stated that ships had to be stopped searched and enemy crews had to be evacuated first before their ship could be sunk, their lifeboats towed towards land before the U-boat could abandon them. However, these Prize Rules robbed the U-boat of its stealth advantage and also opened them up to attack by converted freighters that carried hidden guns to attack surfaced U-boats, the so-called 'Q-ships'. These ships would stop when ordered by a U-boat and a small portion of the crew evacuate in lifeboats before the closing U-boat was attacked by the hidden weaponry.

Meanwhile aboard *U-604* the sinking of the steamer was reported by radio to BdU as part of the normal onboard routine:

> 20.15 hours on 2.12.1942. Single funnel passenger ship, general course 180°, speed 17 knots, sunk in grid square BE 1739. Survivors state 16,000 BRT. 11+2, only 110 cubic metres. Höltring.

After the war it became clear that Höltring had sunk an American ship named *Coamo*, which was also much smaller than claimed. While the survivors informed Höltring that the ship was 16,000 BRT it was in fact 7,057 BRT. The British Admiralty had allowed *Coamo* to leave the comparative shelter of convoy MKF 3, situated 150 miles west of Ireland, and sail independently. They reasoned that the high speed of 17.5 knots would make torpedo attack difficult for a type VIIC as it could outpace the U-boat. This combined with a zigzag course convinced the Admiralty that the steamers safety was guaranteed.

The *Coamo* was launched in 1925 from the Newport News Shipbuilding & Dry Dock Co. The owner this time was Agwilines Inc. from New York, which also became the ship's home port. Nels Helgesen was captain of the *Coamo*.

Helgesen was from the small town of Haugesund that lay on the west Norwegian coast and hosted a small shipyard. Thus Helgesen became fascinated at an early age by shipping, departing in 1905 at the age of seventeen to America to begin a career in the merchant navy. In 1918 he captained his first ship when

The *Coamo* in peacetime. At the outbreak of war she received an overall grey paint scheme.
(With the kind permission of Captain Henry Helgesen)

thirty years old, beginning a career as captain of liners for the New York and Porto Rico Lines. During this career he captained fifteen ships and was featured in a report in the *New York Times* when he set a new speed record aboard *Coamo* running between Puerto Rico and New York.[38] This voyage was completed in 80 hours and 30 minutes – seven and a half hours shorter than the previous record. It was the *Coamo*'s respectable top speed that had allowed this, and that also convinced the Admiralty of its safety in wartime.

At the outbreak of war Helgesen continued in command of *Coamo* and in January 1942 rescued seventy-one survivors from the Canadian ship *Lady Hawkins* that had been sunk by a U-boat. While returning to port *Coamo* nearly rammed a surfaced U-boat, though the latter was able to make a successful crash-dive to safety. By spring the *Coamo* was being used as a troopship and had been armed with one 4-inch cannon, two 3-inch cannon and six 20 mm quick-firing cannon.

On the first journey Helgesen took *Coamo* from Charlston, South Carolina, to South America and from there to Africa, eventually returning to South America and finally Baltimore. During the entire voyage *Coamo* had no enemy contact at all. Possibly it was on these grounds that Helgesen volunteered for one last voyage in this capacity before fresh tasks were assigned; this was the journey when *U-604* sank *Coamo*. The fate of those aboard the *Coamo* if sunk was stark as only fifteen lifeboats were carried. It is unclear whether Captain Helgesen made it into one of the fifteen lifeboats, or how many survivors did, as from the entire complement aboard, no trace was ever found by the Allies. With a bad weather front closing on the area within the next day and in the winter temperatures the survivors stood no chance. Previously, in the Spring, Captain Helgesen has said in an interview about his rescue of the shipwrecked of the *Lady Hawkins*:

I was there for the shipwrecked Canadians, I just hope someone will be there for me when my time comes!

Unfortunately on the day of 2 December 1942 when *U-604* sank *Coamo* there was no one there for them in the North Atlantic.

The merchant navy contingent of the *Coamo* crew was 122 men and 11 officers. There were also 37 gunners and 16 US Army personnel aboard, making 186 souls altogether. None survived. It was the largest loss of life for the American Merchant Navy of World War Two.

At 00.51 hours on 3 December *U-604* received the following radio message:

1 Group 'Draufgänger' in patrol line, Höltring busy in southern position. Other boats return to positions to the north.
2 Höltring report, a ship, possibly troop transport and many shipwrecked sighted, why is your boat so far south . . .

U-604 answered at 04.00 hours:

1 Troop transporter possible, overall grey colour scheme, however not many shipwrecked. About 15 rafts.
2 Boat came 100 nautical miles to the south during hunt. Höltring.

During the following day nothing out of the ordinary was noted. Only the daily test dive broke on the routine. On 4 December *U-604* reached the reported area of the Draufgänger Group and Höltring placed both diesels on slow ahead to conserve fuel. For two days the same routine was followed as lookouts scoured the surrounding seas and radio transmissions monitored for information relayed by German cryptanalytical department about convoy traffic from east and west.

The patrol line stood over the allotted area as this message came in:

05.12.1942 around 14.57 hours. Group Draufgänger. Starting from 6 Decembers 09.00 hours convoy circuit 'Diana' with same times used for the first time . . .
06.12.1942 around 18.16 hours. Group Draufgänger 19.00 hours in the reconnaissance strip head course west, speed 7 knots. On 7 December, 11.00 hours, turn to course east, speed 7 knots.
07.12.1942 around 17.50 hours:
1 Tomorrow at 17.00 hours in new patrol line stand from Grid square AK 2564 to 2994. Operation against eastbound convoy, that on 7 December

around 12.00 hours was sighted in Grid AK 4189, course 50° to 70°, speed
around 8 knots.
2 Immediately America 1 switch 3..
07.12.1942 around 21.51 hours. Draufgänger. Instruction about patrol line
finished . . .Travel in such a way that matches calculated daily distance
covered by convoy.

On 8 December the situation suddenly changed when *U-604* was forced to
make a crash-dive by the sudden appearance of an enemy aircraft. Twenty minutes
after diving, at 17.15 hours, five detonations of aerial bombs were plainly heard
aboard the boat. By 17.35 hours the aircraft had left and *U-604* surfaced and
resumed its course until suddenly to the east the convoy HX 217 came into sight
before the boat was forced under once more by aircraft, emerging from cloud
cover at 1,000 metres.

Convoys with the HX prefix were fast ones originating in Halifax, Nova
Scotia, bound for the United Kingdom. One hour and fifteen minutes after being
forced to dive, *U-604* emerged and sent the following message:

08.12.1942 at 19.55 hours. 18.40 hours Convoy sighted AK 2546, 45°, 9
knots, Alarm dive for 'Consolidated', contact lost.

But within half an hour of surfacing Metox detected radar impulses and the
boat submerged once more until 22.10 hours when it emerged again and homed
in on the presumed general course steered by HX 217. In fact during the
following day *U-604* was forced under twice by enemy radar contact, which led
Höltring to believe that he was in the vicinity of the target merchant ships. The
intensifying air cover would without doubt make any attack approach difficult and
BdU began to have doubts about the boat's ability to operate, briefly ordering the
chase called off. However, this order was rescinded shortly thereafter as is shown
in the following radio traffic:

09.12.1942 around 09.42 hours instruction number 752. Panzer and
Draufgänger. 1) Boats operating in daylight against convoy to break off. Still
take chance to attack if in favourable position.
09.12.1942 around 11.57 hours. Panzer and Draufgänger amendment.
Instruction number 752 thus settled.
09.12.1942 around 12.15 hours. Panzer and Draufgänger. 1) Operate on
Thurmann's message. Probably eastern course, is possibly new convoy.

It lasted until 10 December at 00.12 hours, when flares were seen to starboard providing a reference point for the convoy's location. Höltring dived to use listening gear but to no avail, whereupon *U-604* emerged and headed 260° towards some distant light traces and star shells. With a course of 90° and at slow speed the boat actually stood directly before the convoy. As *U-604* lay in wait listening, thirteen depth–charge explosions were heard. But the boat's position before the convoy transpired to be very unfavourable, because the convoy sailed from the darkness while *U-604* was bathed in bright moonlight. Thus *U-604* turned away onto a course of 160° and Metox once more announced the presence of enemy radar.

A destroyer was the assumed source, sighted shortly afterward at 2,000–metre range. *U-604* increased speed to distance itself from the destroyer. Höltring wanted to let the convoy pass, since he had been pushed so far away by the destroyer. He reasoned that he could have broken through the escort cordon from behind but this plan was beyond the boat's capabilities.

Radio message from *U-604* to 10 December:

05.05 hours. Guidance number 714. 02.46 hours escort in Grid square A 3633, course east, speed 9 knots. Pushed away by destroyers. Feeling lost. Höltring.

Within four hours dawn had broken and the hunt had to be broken off. The radio message received from BdU was:

16.18 hours. Panzer and Draufgänger with all means, despite air cover, try to advance in order to attack during the coming night. Now is the last chance.

Nevertheless the boat was able to maintain distant contact with the convoy, with the smoke trails of many funnels being just visible. Twice more *U-604* was forced under by hostile aircraft, and Höltring radioed that day:

12 00 hours. Briefly sighted distant smoke cloud AL 1648. Then constantly pushed under by air cover. No further contact. Höltring

During the following night, BdU ordered the pursuit broken off. Fuel reserves on *U-604* had shrunk from 136 m^3 to 75 m^3, but once again a fresh convoy sighting was reported.

16.51 hours. Höltring on 13 December 20.00 hours in patrol line from . . . west going convoy starting from 14 December in the morning. These boats to form Ungestüm group . . .

The Ungestüm group comprised *U-336* (Hunger), *U-373* (Loeser), *U-435* (Strelow), *U-445* (Fenn), *U-455* (Scheibe), *U-524* (Steinacker), *U-569* (Hinsch), *U-591* (Zetz), *U-604* (Höltring), *U-615* (Kapitzky) and *U-628* (Hasenschar). Apart from *U-524*, which was a type IXC U-boat, the remainder were all VIICs. *U-604* altered course to 245° and increased speed to take its position. The following day, distant ASDIC was detected while submerged, seemingly originating from two separate sources, hence Höltring deduced two destroyers. *U-604* reached its new position at 06.00 hours on 13 December. But once again, not one ship of the westbound convoy ON 152 was to be seen. Only the searching sound of two destroyers was noted. Höltring assumed that they belonged to the Escort Group C-3, which guarded ON 152. BdU thereupon instructed:

19.34 hours. Group Ungestüm from Hunger to Steinacker and Höltring, proceed to the west. On 15 December at around 00.00 position in new patrol line at . . .
21.12 hours . . . in the instructed Ungestüm patrol line, Höltring holds the southern position . . .

The convoy, on which the two groups Ungestüm and Büffel now concentrated, was HX 218 which was escorted by Escort Group B-3. Although a fast convoy – as opposed to those prefixed 'SC' for Slow Convoy – the two types shared the same transatlantic routes from Halifax to the United Kingdom.

During the afternoon on 15 December, *U-604* was forced to submerge by enemy aircraft and the distant sound of screw noises could be heard at 140°, which Höltring pursued at full speed once he surfaced again after forty minutes. He reported the contact to BdU as hopes were raised aboard *U-604* that the hunt seemed on again. However, the seemingly ever-present aircraft repeatedly forced *U-604* to dive, frustrating its ability to give chase. Although this aerial threat usefully marked proximity to the convoy, it also posed a grave threat, and after the second crash-dive seven bombs followed *U-604* under water, though doing no damage. By 19.03 hours *U-604* surfaced again and charged ahead in pursuit. This time a sinister destroyer emerging from a rain squall would frustrate the chase. It was some 6,000 metres away so did not notice the U-boat; as a result no depth-charges followed the boat as it sank into the depths again. The boat emerged again around 20.00 hours. Radio messages received aboard *U-604* on 15 December recorded the chase:

19.53 hours. Ungestüm . . . 11.00 hours in morning patrol line stand from grid AK 2842 to 6434.
21.35 hours. Höltring searches alone, and occupies no position in the patrol line . . .

Höltring's contribution to the radio traffic followed shortly thereafter:

21.45 hours, AK 5194, twice aircraft, Flibos, 1939 forced under by destroyer, no more sound detection, last sound approximately 90° at 21.00 hours . . .

The next two days passed unexpectedly calmly. No hostile activities, no convoy. Fog arose and the sea became ever more rough; on the morning of 16 December at strength 4 and by evening strength 6. Life aboard a surfaced U-boat was difficult in such seas, especially in the bow room that accommodated the majority of the crew. This bow compartment was always first to bury itself in high seas, pitching alarmingly. Additionally, the lookouts had an arduous time, having to attach themselves with heavy belts and lines in order not to be washed overboard. On other U-boats men had been lost when had not done this; once an entire bridge watch was found to be missing when the relief watch climbed the conning tower ladder.

The chief engineer aboard *U-604* had another problem as a result of the storm: the uneven strain on the diesels. Every time the propellers drove through a mountainous wave and emerged in fresh air the revolutions jumped alarmingly, before being suddenly slowed by water resistance as they were plunged once again under water. This irregularity was torture for the diesel engines, and although the solution was to submerge in such harsh conditions to 30 metres where the swell was no longer evident, this could only be done for a relatively short period due to the battery capacity. For this and more prosaic operational reasons Höltring pressed on surfaced, submerging only to listen on hydrophones for possible convoy noises. But the enemy ships seemed to have disappeared.

The weather continued to worsen, at strength 8 on 17 December and reaching 9 and gale-like conditions the following day. The conditions were so severe that without warning an enemy destroyer emerged from the blinding rain at a distance of only 200 metres, though it failed to notice the U-boat before it disappeared just as quickly. Perhaps the Allied crew had enough on their hands dealing with the conditions as well. Delivery of an attack in those conditions would have been virtually impossible at any rate. BdU next informed the boats of the Ungestüm group that refuelling was unavailable and therefore any boats low on fuel could begin their return voyage. Two days later *U-604* detected screw noises once more and followed the contact hoping to regain the enemy but to no avail. Only *U-*

455 obtained contact. The storm had abated by this stage to a strength 4 and life became more bearable aboard the boats.

However, its effect was still felt aboard *U-604* as the radio transmitter had been disabled, a precarious situation for a U-boat in action. Funkmaat Georg Seitz was tasked with finding the problem. First all amplifier tubes of the radio transmitter were examined to check they were functional, as were the various power packs. With no trace of malfunction Seitz was faced with the possibility that the transmitting antenna itself was faulty. He climbed to the bridge and examined the antenna, which trailed along the forward net deflector jumper wire. There the problem was found: the connection from the tower lining to the actual antenna had been damaged in the severe weather. However, with seas still rough it seemed that repair would be almost impossible. But there was no choice. Seitz was secured with a rope and lowered down the outside of the conning tower. It was a delicate affair, as he tried not to be swept overboard, but the task went smoothly and the transmitter was repaired. The following two days were uneventful as the convoy eluded *U-604* and finally Höltring turned for home, his fuel at its limit.

22.12.1942. 07.43 hours. BD 1717. Begin return journey. 28 m³ fuel.

With only 20 per cent of its fuel remaining *U-604* headed for Brest, celebrating Christmas Eve three days later. The cook manufactured some cakes despite his limited supplies and space and the men even managed to construct a tree for the occasion.

In the long quiet phases between convoy attacks or attacks on single sailing ships, there was also time for completely unrelated activities aboard the U-boat. This poem written by Funkmaat Georg Seitz shows a beautiful view of this somewhat surreal period of calm, written during this third war patrol.

Atlantic tragedy – 1942
By the Atlantic night,
Calmly trace their course
A hundred strong Greenland whales
And the largest swims in front.

On the Atlantic night,
Drive faster their course,
Ten to twenty grey boats,
With feeling in front too.

Above: The make-shift Christmas tree, on the right viewed from the Zentrale.
Below: The crew celebrate Christmas: Commandant Höltring is in the black sweater.

Under the Atlantic night,
Radio operators listen keenly to GHG,
Announce constantly, 'Strong signals!'
But the enemy is not seen.

In the Atlantic space,
Diesels run 'full speed',
Behind a herd of whales,
What kind of hunt is this?

On the Atlantic night,
A new life begins.
Instead of tankers,
One hunts whales.

On 26 December a steamer surprisingly came into view, but Höltring was unable to give chase. The ship ran at 17 knots and with little fuel aboard *U-604* there was no chance of pursuit. The contact was radioed to BdU and *U-604* carried on undeterred.

Höltring continued for the remainder of his return surfaced at night and submerged by day to minimise risk of air attack. On 31 December he rendezvoused with his escort and at 08.37 hours the boat fastened to the pier in Brest. Some of the crew were later awarded the Iron Cross, 2nd Class, for their third war patrol.

Statement from BdU written in the War Diary for U-604 *covering the period from 3 November to 31 December 1942*

During pursuit and sinking the high-speed single ship on 2 December the commander acted skilfully. On the other hand, during the operation on the convoy of 8–10 December there could have been greater chance of success. The boat had several opportunities but because of unfavourable attack conditions, brief frustration by a destroyer and because of submerging before detection, there was no chance for attack. Chances at convoys are rare and all possibilities must therefore be seized even in unfavourable conditions. Appreciative success: 1 ship with 12,000 BRT sunk.

On its third war patrol *U-604* sank the *Coamo* on 2 December 1942; its tonnage was entered in German records erroneously. Shipwrecked survivors told Höltring it was 16,000 BRT, BdU revised this to 12,000 BRT, but in fact it was 7,057 BRT. In *U-604*'s third war patrol and the period spent preparing for the fourth patrol the following U-boats were sunk by the allies (26 November 1942–7 February 1943)

1	*U-611*	Jakobs †	sunk on	08.12.1942
2	*U-626*	Bade†	sunk on	15.12.1942
3	*U-357*	Kellner †	sunk on	26.12.1942
4.	*U-356*	Ruppelt †	sunk on	27.12.1942
5	*U-553*	Thurmann †	sunk on	02.01.1943
6	*U-164*	Fechner	sunk on	06.01.1943
7	*U-224*	Kosbadt †	sunk on	13.01.1943
8	*U-507*	Schacht †	sunk on	13.01.1943
9	*U-337*	Ruwiedel †	sunk on	15.01.1943
10	*U-301*	Korner †	sunk on	21.01.1943
11	*U-265*	Auffhammer †	sunk on	03.02.1943
12	*U-187*	Munnich †	sunk on	04.02.1943
13	*U-609*	Rudloff †	sunk on	07.02.1943
14	*U-624*	Frauenhofen †	sunk on	07.02.1943

Index †: Captain killed in the sinking.

U-604 had been with *U-609* during their first war patrol as part of the Vorwärts group.

Track Chart of the Third War Patrol
  Sea–days of the third enemy trip: 36 days
  Round trip distance: 5.649.5 nautical miles

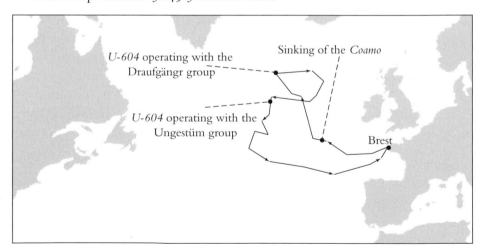

Funkmaat Georg Seitz receives his EK II.

Sinking pennant for *Coamo* with the
presumed tonnage.

The Fourth War Patrol

U-604 had lain in the Brest yards from New Year's Day 1943 to 7 February, beginning its fourth patrol the following day at 16.02 hours into the waters of Biscay that were blown by wind to sea state 5. Two other boats departed France that same day, *U-659* among them, alongside which *U-604* had ended its second patrol in Brest. Altogether sixty-nine boats sailed into the North Atlantic in February 1943; eight of these would never return and sixteen were forced to break off operations prematurely. Of the total number, thirty-two were on their maiden patrols.[39] That month U-boats would sink sixty-seven ships totalling 362,081 BRT, the figure rising in March to 110 ships totalling 633, 731 BRT.[40]

At this time the Axis powers had achieved an enormous advantage in their radio coding system. German military and police units used the code machine Enigma in several variants. Starting on 1 February 1943 Dönitz had ordered all U-boat Enigma machines to be equipped with a fourth rotor and a new code key, named 'Triton'. Although Enigma had been compromised earlier in the war, this new system blocked Allied decoding efforts and thus the Allies were blinded once more to German U-boat movements. Additionally, German radio listening stations had successfully breached the Allied 'Naval Number 3' code used in convoy operations. Thus as *U-604* sailed the initiative in this covert war passed to the Kriegsmarine.[41]

As Höltring sailed into Biscay, Metox detected enemy aircraft radar at 23.58 hours on 9 February and forced the first crash-dive. Thereafter Höltring travelled submerged by day and surfaced by night, averaging only 140 nautical miles a day with the reduced underwater speed available.

During such submerged travel depth-charge explosions were heard, estimated at 50 miles distant and the following day at 08.48 hours screw noises were detected at 340°. Again depth-charges were also heard, on the same bearing and closer at an estimated 20 to 50 nautical miles. The screw noises grew steadily louder and *U-604* faced the risk of detection by ASDIC and entanglement in a lengthy depth-

A Focke Wulf Condor on Atlantic patrol. (With kind permission of Bibliothek für Zeitgeschichte)

charge hunt. Therefore Höltring opted to surface and run at high speed to the south despite the daylight. For two hours *U-604* headed at high speed away from the enemy before diving once more. However, screw noises and depth-charges were still audible, this time estimated to be 30 miles away.

Four hours later, around 20.30 hours on 11 February, new screw noises were detected at 202° followed later by the chilling sound of ASDIC. There was no doubt that the ship was an enemy ASW vessel and once more Höltring opted to surface and use his high diesel speed, gradually leaving the feared Biscay 'Valley of Death' behind. Only the daily test dives interrupted the U-boat's passage as it received instructions from BdU to make for grid squares AL and AK for new operations. Altogether thirty-two submarines were to gather in three new groups: Knappen, Neptun and Ritter. *U-604* was assigned to Knappen. Knappen and Ritter together consisted of fourteen boats. For two of the boats the operation was immediately disastrous, both *U-529* (Fraatz) and *U-225* (Leimkühler) were sunk, although the groups had not yet encountered enemy convoy traffic, suggesting that the Allies had pinpointed their positions using direction-finding or radar. How *U-529* was sunk remains unknown; *U-225* was sunk by an RAF aeroplane.[42] On 18 February there was still no convoy contact, only a Luftwaffe Focke Wulf FW-200 Condor reporting a convoy heading west.[43] Luftwaffe reconnaissance in the Atlantic rarely matched expectations; too few aircraft, and tolerances in navigation between the U-boats at sea and Luftwaffe reports hugely different. The Luftwaffe were simply not accurate enough to vector U-boats towards the enemy and served generally as little more than vague indicators.

Since the reported convoy was some distance from the gathering boats, a new group, Burggraf, was formed by five U-boats from Knappen. *U-604*, however, remained as part of the latter and continued to search the presumed course of the

The *Stockport*, showing its Huff-Duff antenna mounted at the masthead.
(With kind permission of Bibliothek für Zeitgeschichte)

original convoy continuing to sail alongside the boats of the Ritter group. At 04.00 hours on 19 February BdU issued instructions to Höltring:

> Oelrich, Höltring, Walkering and Zurmühlen form group Knappen and from 00.00 hours 20 February occupy patrol line from AK 9295 to 9684. Westbound convoy expected 20 February. From 08.00 hours 19 February switch to Diana.

Funkmaat Georg Seitz announced at 08.50 hours on 20 February screw noises at 20°. Höltring dived to follow the sound and thus *U-604* became contact boat against the 40 ships of convoy ON 166.[44] The prefix ON stood for Outbound North, fast convoys heading from the United Kingdom back to America. Slow-running convoys would use the same route but be designated ONS. Escort Group A-3 was tasked with protecting the ships, comprising eight warships, USS *Spencer* and HMS *Campbell* both carrying radar and Huff-Duff, and five further corvettes and the rescue ship *Stockport* carrying Huff-Duff alone.[45] *Stockport* had already experienced action, rescuing over 300 people from torpedoed ships.

Höltring transmitted his progress to BdU:

> Possible escort screws broad volume, very quiet. Höltring

The US Coast Guard cutter USS *Spencer*, part of the escort for ON 166.
(With kind permission of Bibliothek für Zeitgeschichte)

11.15 hours. Grid AK 9613 enemy in sight to starboard . . . Very poor
visibility . . . With full speed running against the sea. Corvette does not
follow. Because of the poor visibility, enemy comes in and out of
sight . . . 1 steamer and 3 corvettes recognised.
11.31 hours. Contact held . . .

From this and the string of instructions that followed nearly twenty U-boats
converged on ON 166 and began what was to become the biggest convoy battle
of the war. *U-604* remained in contact with the convoy awaiting permission to
attack and guiding the other boats towards the enemy. The escort ships had gained
considerable experience over the previous years and made the task of shadowing
very difficult for *U-604*, often pushing the boat out of visible contact. Also *U-604*
was exposed to the danger of radio direction-finding as constant messages flowed
from Seitz's radio cabin. An escort vehicle equipped with Huff-Duff could
quickly locate the source of the transmission and home in on its bearing. The
bridge lookouts were therefore exhorted extreme vigilance at this delicate stage

Sailing alongside *U-462*.

of the hunt to prevent surprise attack.

The Ritter group comprised the following boats: *U-332* (Ritter), *U-377* (Köbler), *U-454* (Hackländer), *U-468* (Schamong), *U-529* (Fraatz), *U-603* (Bertelsmann), *U-623* (Schröder), *U-628* (Hasenschar), *U-653* (Feiler), *U-753* (Mannstein). Knappen comprised *U-91* (Walkering), *U-92* (Oelrich), *U-600* (Zurmühlen) and *U-604* (Höltring). Also operating in the region were *U-186* (Hesemann), *U-223* (Wächter), *U-303* (Heine), *U-621* (Kruschka) and *U-707* (Gretschel) possibly as parts of the Neptun or Büffel groups.

U-604 announced by short signal on 20 February:

Enemy stands Grid AK 9618, course 240°, speed 7 knots.
Enemy stands Grid AK 9563, course 230°, speed 7 knots.

The messages travelled back and forth as BdU attempted to glean more information from Höltring about the convoy composition, until finally:

19.15 hours. To Höltring: attack freely as soon as further boats announce contact. Continue to send bearings.

It became apparent that Höltring was still the sole contact with ON 166, and in difficult visibility conditions. He decided to follow the escort ships since they operated on a parallel course to the convoy until more U–boats were available. Occasionally *U-604* disappeared, submerging to verify convoy location with listening gear. At 21.30 hours the convoy came once more into sight, *U-604* lying almost directly in its path as the convoy had turned south. He reasoned that he could penetrate the escort screen of the front sweepers, but still Höltring was unable to attack as no new U-boats had been reported. Höltring continued to shadow, but inevitably was detected. USS *Spencer* fixed the boat with radar and *U-604* was forced to make a crash-dive as the American dropped five depth-charges, though with no major effect.[46] After a further five minutes more depth-charges followed and Höltring spent two hours under water before surfacing. Although no real damage had been suffered, the *Spencer* had succeeded. On 21 February he transited to BdU:

04.00 hours. Submerged due to destroyer, depth-charges. Last convoy sighting 01.04 hours, grid QU 9885, course 180°, speed 8 knots. No contact. Höltring.

In the meantime BdU lifted the attack restriction as *U-332* (Hüttemann) and *U-603* (Bertelsmann) had both contacted ON 166. They found the convoy from Höltring's bearing transmissions and once Höltring had surfaced they repaid the favour by bringing *U-604* back in contact at around 09.56 hours. The lookouts aboard *U-604* sighted smoke at 201° and were forced under water shortly afterwards by enemy aircraft. However, this allowed listening detection of the convoy screw noises, estimated at a distance of 20 to 30 nautical miles. Within the hour the boat was surfaced and heading at high speed towards ON 166. But the boat was forced once more to submerge by a prowling Liberator, this time unfortunate mechanical problems forcing a delay in continuing the chase.

21.02.1943 at 14.28 hours. Surfaced . . . frequent small diesel breakdowns. Attributed to poor shipyard work. For example from starboard shock mounting strong lubricating oil loss since housing screws turned only once and not tightened. Maximum speed cannot be made from this.

U-604 was also not the only boat attacked on this day by an aeroplane. *U-623* Schröder was also attacked likewise and posted missing thereafter. *U-454* and *U-91* were also aerially depth-charged but survived.[47] The Allies knew that a large number of U-boats had gathered against ON 166 and strengthened the escort with the Polish destroyer ORP *Burza* which had been tasked with escorting ON 167.[48]

Half an hour later *U-604* received messages from the current contact boat *U-454* (Hackländer):

21.02.1943 at 15.00 hours. More smoke clouds sighted BD3457. Fairly scattered. From Hackländer.

The Polish destroyer *Burza* (left) and its sister ship.
(With kind permission of Bibliothek für Zeitgeschichte)

21.02.1943 at 18.14 hours. 16.10 hours convoy after smoke clouds. Grid 3476. Forced underwater by destroyer and air.

U-604 continued to home in on ON 166 although the lookouts sighted no trace of smoke. However at about this time the first ship of the convoy was sunk. It was the 5,964-ton *Stigsand*, torpedoed by *U-332* and damaged before being finished off by *U-603*.[49] The largest convoy battle had begun. Höltring, mean-while, dived and at 21.14 hours the sound man detected twenty-five depth-charge explosions in the middle distance. It was USS *Spencer* sinking *U-225* and Höltring surfaced and immediately headed for the source of the noise. In the meantime there was a second U-boat, *U-92*, in contact and attacking:

23.00 hours. Convoy at 22.30 hours in grid BD 5326, course 240°, 6 knots, 7,000 BRT sunk. 2 failures. 85 m³ fuel. No wind. Ölrich[50]

On the night of 21 February and up to late evening the following day more boats began to attack ON 166. *U-92* and *U-753* unintentionally torpedoed the same ship, the 9,348-ton *Nielsen Alonso*, which nonetheless refused to sink. The *Campbell* sheered away from escort duty momentarily and rescued fifty crewmen from the stricken vessel. *U-753* in turn was so heavily damaged by depth-charge retaliation that the boat was forced to break off and head home.[51] *U-606* (Döhler) torpedoed and sank the 5,687-ton *Chattanooga City* and damaged American freighter *Expositor* and British freighter *Empire Redshank*. The latter was sunk by a British corvette using cannon fire so that the convoy could continue in formation.[52] The *Expositor* was finished off by *U-303* Heine later that night, its original damage relatively minor.

Nevertheless *U-606* paid a high price for its success. It was located and hunted by USS *Chilliwack*, ORP *Burza* and the *Campbell*, damaged by depth-charge and forced to the surface where it came under sustained cannon fire. The *Campbell* turned and immediately rammed the U-boat, riding over the U-boat, which resulted in a 4-metre crack in its own hull. As the Germans abandoned ship, gunfire killed many so that from fifty men only twelve were rescued. The *Burza* took onboard the men from *Nielsen Alonso* that Campbell had saved as well as twelve of the crewmen from *U-606* and a small part of the crew of the *Campbell*. The ship was then towed under escort protection to Newfoundland.[53]

After midnight *U-604* proceeded relatively slowly surfaced, and the lookout sighted a destroyer 5 miles away almost directly ahead. A short time later a second destroyer was sighted to starboard at 6 miles, although both disappeared from view. At around 02.24 hours the port diesel failed and *U-604* could only proceed slowly after the convoy. Hours later the lookouts sighted the enormous smoke cloud of a burning steamer which Höltring elected to finish off. Before he could, however, the Polish destroyer *Burza* emerged, took fifty men off the burning ship and sank it with a torpedo. The *Burza* then immediately retreated, heading to St John's. The corvette *Dianthus* had also been forced to break away due to lack of fuel which left the escort reduced to five ships while sixteen U-boats still operated against the convoy.

Höltring continued to broadcast information to BdU on 22 February:

02.47 hours. Grid BD 5237 12.20 hours estimated 5,000 tons sunk by destroyer *Burza*. From Höltring.

In the meantime *U-604* operated against a solo sailing ship that had been reported by *U-753*. But it could not be found all day long and even underwater listening failed to reveal any trace of it to the men aboard *U-604*. Elsewhere other

The corvette *Dianthus.* (With kind permission of Bibliothek für Zeitgeschichte)

U-boats were also apparently having problems regaining contact with the main convoy.

It was morning on 23 February, around 03.04 hours, before the bridge watch sighted a steamer at a distance of 2,500 metres. The ship was steering a course of 230° at 12 knots and Höltring immediately steered hard to starboard and attacked. He fired a four torpedo salvo at 03.12 hours. Two hits were registered and within three minutes the steamer had sunk after an explosion deep within its hull.

Höltring estimated its size at 7,000 BRT and radioed on 23 February:

> 03.41 hours. Grid 4633. Passenger steamer 7,000 BRT sunk. 240° course, 11 knots. 8 + 2, 72 m³. SW to W, 4–5, sea state 4, meaning high swell, strongly changing visibility. Rain showers . . . Höltring.

U-604 had sunk the *Stockport*, the rescue ship from ON 166. She had rescued men from the *Empire Trade*, damaged by *U-92*, later transferring them to the HMCS *Dauphin*, after which she had dropped back behind the convoy and become an easy target for *U-604*.[54] The *Stockport* was far from 7,000 BRT, only displacing 1,683 BRT and at this time already an ageing vessel. She had been built in 1911 by the Earle's Shipbuilding & Engineering Co. Ltd in Hull. Its home port was Grimsby and it was owned by the London & North Eastern Railway Company. On 22 October 1942 *Stockport* was taken into service as a rescue ship by the Royal Navy and had travelled as part of sixteen convoys and rescued at least 430 men from various sunken ships. Its last journey had begun on 8 February 1943 from Greenock, Scotland, travelling first to the Clyde and then on 11 February into the Atlantic as part of ON 166 headed for St John's. From the sixty-four men aboard when she was torpedoed, none survived.

After sinking the *Stockport* U-604 attempted once more to operate against the convoy. First, though, the boat was dived to allow the four bow tubes to be reloaded. While the torpedo crew laboured, loud destroyer noises were detected to port; Höltring later followed these traces, but all contact was lost. Other boats were in a better position than *U-604* to attack the convoy: *U-303* sank the 4,959-ton *Expositor*; *U-223* the 6,907-ton *Winkler*; *U-186* the 5,401-ton *Hastings* and the 6,207-ton *Eulima*; *U-603* the 6,409-ton Norwegian *Glittre*.[55]

Radio messages continued to be received onboard *U-604* both from BdU exhorting the boats to attack under water by day should the weather situation permit, by speeding ahead to lay in the convoy path. Also, sighting reports from U-boats still in contact continued to flow toward BdU's situation room. On the same day as *U-604* sailed surfaced, a cutter with a red sail was sighted. Shortly thereafter Höltring issued the following radio message:

23.12 hours. Request at next opportunity resupply of new cable for Fu.M.B. Old one totally useless. From Höltring.

The Metox cable had failed and now the U-boat had lost the ability to scan for enemy radar signals. This placed *U-604* in substantially increased danger, because now it was only the lookouts with their binoculars that could detect any incoming threat from aircraft attack in a sky still heavy with covering cloud. It was not for nothing that U-boat crews claimed that 'a good lookout is half of life!' But, although difficult to spot by day, at night there was little chance in seeing an attacking aircraft armed with radar and Leigh Light until the blinding beam straddled the target U-boat. Höltring had to exercise extreme caution now in order to minimise the danger to his boat and crew. Even with a clear blue sky there remained a risk as hostile aircraft made every attempt to attack from out of the blinding glare of the sun.

But the night passed relatively calmly for Höltring, while elsewhere four boats successfully attacked ON 166. *U-707* sank its first ship that night, the 7,176-ton Liberty *Jonathan Sturges*. Commander Feiler aboard *U-653* sank two ships though

  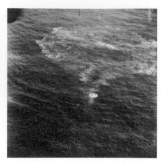

The unsuccessful attack on *U-604* from the Allied perspective. The explosion of the depth-charge aimed at it is shown vividly. (With kind permission of USAF Historical Research Agency USAFHRC-2595-494 and 498)

they were initially unconfirmed; the British *Delilian* and Dutch *Madoera* and in the early morning hours *U-628* sank 4,391-ton Norwegian ship *Ingra*.[56]

By this stage the convoy had reached a position far enough west to receive additional air cover from Catalinas stationed on Newfoundland. Four aircraft were despatched to provide air cover for the remains of ON 166. That day *U-604* submerged to listen for screw noises and emerged shortly afterward, 900 kilometres from Newfoundland. It was there that the lack of Metox became profoundly evident as the boat was attacked by a Catalina.

At around 14.17 hours the Catalina dropped four bombs on the boat, though fortunately for Höltring they were inaccurate and caused no significant damage. Happily the pilot had dropped his bombs wide and *U-604* made a rapid crash-dive to escape as a second salvo exploded behind it.

Aboard *U-604* although there had been no mortal damage but there remained myriad defects following the near miss, the most serious being bent diesel couplings to the main clutches that could not be fully disengaged, and a half-metre tear in diving cell number 5. Nevertheless, the boat was still functional and Höltring steered a course of 50° for the necessary repair work to be undertaken. My research has shown that the Catalina was flown by Canadian Flight Lieutenant F. C. Colborne, who had started his patrol from Newfoundland at around 07.45 hours Canadian time. His brief was to help protect ON 166 acting as air escort and reconnaissance.[57]

Höltring's next radio transmission was sent on 24 February:

16.51 hours. BC 9225. Heavy Flibos. Foundations of both compressors damaged. Water coolant flange leaking strongly. Diving cell 5 damaged. Not clear for deep dives. Set off to repair. Höltring.

A few days later Höltring wrote the following remark in the war diary:

> No reproach on Seaman Number One for late sighting of the enemy
> machine since it came out of strong cloud layer and was only recognised
> with the naked eye after the port-front sector was searched with binoculars.

Throughout the remainder of 24 February the crew of *U-604* were occupied
with repairs, while the remaining boats continued to attack the convoy. By
midnight the compressor foundations had been welded, although the coolant
valves continued to leak strongly. Höltring suspected that stud nuts had not been
properly secured during the boat's last shipyard stay and had been broken by the
detonations. Thus coolant continue to leak and *U-604* was eventually forced to
concede and begin the homeward trek on 26 February at 00.05 hours. That same
day BdU called off the hunt of ON 166:

> 01.27 hours. Tomorrow as dawn breaks break off attack on convoy. Tonight
> is the last chance. Afterward report location, fuel and ammunition levels and
> head for Grid BD 81. Only exceed the 100 metre line if there are good
> attack prospects.

U-604 was, in February 1943, only one of seventeen boats which had to begin
the journey home through damage. The convoy now lay directly off
Newfoundland in much too shallow waters. With less than 100 metres under the
hull, U-boats would have had little chance of escaping a sustained depth-charge
pursuit. Nonetheless, despite Dönitz's order to cease operations the U-boats had
claimed a successful tally: fourteen ships with a combined tonnage of 87,901 BRT
sunk. Considering that the complete convoy consisted of forty ships, the U-boats
had destroyed 35 per cent of the entire convoy. The total losses to the Allies were
heavier still when those ships that had been damaged were taken into account.[58]
In response the Allies sank four U-boats. One of the largest convoy battles was
over. The British Admiralty recorded that:

> The enemy had never before shown such determination with the
> employment of his power.

U-604 reported against to BdU on 26 February:

> 11.32 hours. Unable to repair diving cell 5. Exhausts 2 and 4 very leaky, thus
> very bad seagoing situation . . . Diesel clutches slipping heavily. Beginning

The *Milchkuh U-Vowe* on 17 February 1943 at the rendezvous with *U-604* in BD 5777.

return voyage. Currently BD 4978. Ask for possible resupply of FuMB cable from supply boat. Höltring.

During the return voyage the boat was barely seaworthy, laying heavy in the water; diving cells 6 and 2 were not watertight and so the boat sailed only with the portside cells watertight, and diving cells 5, 3 and half of cell 1 flooded to keep the boat on as even a keel as possible. Höltring remarked on the convoy battle within the boat's war diary:

> Finally, as far as the convoy operation is concerned, the boat would certainly have managed to get the convoy if it hadn't been held up by frequent diesel repairs preventing us from using maximum speed and furthermore by the destroyer on 22.02, the accidentally discovered steamer on 22.02 and having to dive to reload during 23.02 all of which held us back.

In the meantime a rendezvous with *U-462*, a *Milchkuh* resupply U-boat, was arranged in Grid Square BD 5777. *U-604* reached the allotted area and searched for signs of the large type XIV U-boat. It was the following day at 14.00 hours that she hove into view. The sea state was low and visibility 6 to 8 miles as the two boats met to transfer material to *U-604*. The Metox cables were duly provided – entering the heavily patrolled waters of Biscay without the aid of Metox would have been extremely hazardous for *U-604*. Coupled with other basic supplies was

The 1WO Siegfried von Rothkirch und Panthen leading his bridge watch. On his cap can be seen a badge of the first emblem used by *U-604*.

also the provision of eight new pairs of binoculars.

After the meeting *U-604* continued homebound, unhampered for the next two days as it headed for Brest. On 3 March while travelling submerged aerial bombs or perhaps a torpedo detonation were heard, the listening gear also picking up the sound of diesel engines. Similar contacts accompanied the boat into Biscay and on 8 March the new Metox announced the approach of three aircraft, Höltring successfully diving to safety before the following day rendezvousing with the German escort craft, tying up to the pier in Brest at 11.30 hours.

The 1 WO, Siegfried von Rothkirch und Panthen, left the boat following this fourth patrol to attend U-boat commander's school. Later he would captain *U-717*, which reached active service in August 1944 where, with no successes, the boat was lost. However, in March 1943 the crew of *U-604* that had returned from their fourth and most difficult patrol thus far had ample cause to celebrate. Two crew members from *U-604* suffered a minor fright from their celebrations: Maschinenmaat Robert Marquardt and Funkmaat Georg Seitz after their fourth war patrol went into Brest as part of the first group let ashore during the early afternoon. After some visits to their local restaurants and the Serviceman's Club in the well-known locality in the Rue de Siam they were considerably worse for wear and tear from cognac consumption that afternoon and evening in the port and found themselves in a stupor clinging to an iron railing. Robert temporarily revived, blinked as his eyes cleared and then started turning deathly pale. Before him swam many large live fish in green seawater, with crabs and mussels also in plain view. Robert's trembling hand groped at his comrade's sleeve as in a trembling voice he said, 'Schorsch . . . now they have us by the arse! We're sunk.' Both were, of course, standing before a huge window, behind it a large marine aquarium.

The track chart for the fourth war patrol
    Sea days for the fourth patrol: 28 days at sea
    Round trip distance: 3,659.6 nautical miles

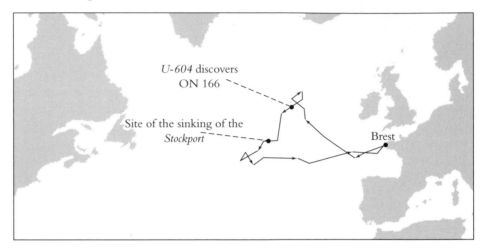

Comment from BdU written in the War Diary for U-604 *covering the period from 1 January–9 March 1943*
    The operation of this commander against the Höltring convoy was unsatisfactory. He was hampered by machinery malfunctions and an initial prohibition on attack, which unfortunately led to his leaving and losing contact. More was expected from this commander during this operation! The return home was begun on account of severe aircraft damage.

On its fourth patrol *U-604* sank the passenger freighter (incorrectly estimated at 7,000 BRT) *Stockport* on 23 February 1943, 1.683 BRT.

In *U-604*'s fourth war patrol and the period spent preparing for the fifth patrol the following U-boats were sunk by the Allies (8 February–21 April 1943):

1	*U-519*	Eppen †	sunk on	10.02.1943
2	*U-442*	Hesse †	sunk on	12.02.1943
3	*U-620*	Stein †	sunk on	13.02.1943
4	*U-529*	Fraatz †	sunk on	15.02.1943
5	*U-225*	Leimkühler †	sunk on	15.02.1943
6	*U-69*	Gräf	sunk on	17.02.1943
7	*U-201*	Rosenberg †	sunk on	17.02.1943
8	*U-205*	Bürgel	sunk on	17.02.1943

9	*U-268*	Heydemann †	sunk on	19.02.1943
10	*U-562*	Hamm †	sunk on	19.02.1943
11	*U-623*	Schröder †	sunk on	21.02.1943
12	*U-606*	Döhler †	sunk on	22.02.1943
13	*U-443*	Puttkamer †	sunk on	23.02.1943
14	*U-522*	Schneider †	sunk on	23.02.1943
15	*U-83*	Wörishoffer †	sunk on	04.03.1943
16	*U-87*	Berger †	sunk on	04.03.1943
17	*U-156*	Hartenstein †	sunk on	08.03.1943
18	*U-633*	Müller †	sunk on	10.03.1943
19	*U-432*	Eckhard †	sunk on	11.03.1943
20	*U-130*	Keller †	sunk on	13.03.1943
21	*U-163*	Engelmann †	sunk on	13.03.1943
22	*U-384*	Rosenburg †	sunk on	20.03.1943
23	*U-524*	Steinacker †	sunk on	22.03.1943
24	*U-665*	Haupt †	sunk on	22.03.1943
25	*U-469*	Claussen †	sunk on	25.03.1943
26	*U-169*	Bauer †	sunk on	27.03.1943
27	*U-77*	Hartmann †	sunk on	28.03.1943
28	*U-416*	Reich	sunk on	30.03.1943
29	*U-124*	Mohr †	sunk on	03.04.1943
30	*U-632*	Karpf	sunk on	06.04.1943
31	*U-635*	Eckelmann †	sunk on	06.04.1943
32	*U-644*	Jensen †	sunk on	07.04.1943
33	*U-376*	Marks †	sunk on	10.04.1943
34	*U-526*	Möglich †	sunk on	14.04.1943
35	*U-175*	Bruns †	sunk on	17.04.1943

†: Commander killed in sinking.

U-604 had operated alongside *U-524* during its third patrol as part of the Ungestüm group.

The Fifth War Patrol

During April 1943 ninety U-boats departed for operations in the North Atlantic, twenty-three of them engaged on their maiden patrols. It marked a high tide for the U-boats: the highest number that had sailed for the North Atlantic in any month of the war. Thirty of these boats would forever be at sea, ten lost on their first voyages.[59] It was a heavy toll on the U-boats and even their score of enemy ships destroyed nowhere near matched previous months, due largely to increasingly effective ASW defences that the Allies had been developing in the meantime. During April 1943 the U-boats sank fifty ships totalling 287,137 BRT.[60]

On 22 April *U-604* departed as the fifty-eighth boat to sail that month, two days later than originally planned. There had been continuing problems with the Junkers compressor that produced the compressed air needed to blow tanks and surface the boat. It was 15.00 hours when the boat finally emerged from the Brest U-boat bunker and ran out into Biscay with *U-621* (Kruschka), who would have better fortune on its war patrol than Höltring as the problems with the compressor were but a foreshadow of the problems that would curtail *U-604*'s fifth patrol. While travelling slowly on the second day from port the engine cylinder compressor tore, causing such heavy damage that it could not be repaired at sea. Höltring was forced to abort and return to base. Besides this, the exhaust valve would not close so that *U-604* could only briefly and shallowly submerge lest the boat be flooded.[61]

U-604 was by no means the only boat to break off a patrol prematurely in April 1943; twenty others were forced to do likewise, fourteen of them due to enemy action. Two had to return after colliding with one another, two accomplished rescue operations and another acted as escort protection for a damaged boat.[62]

During the voyage home a crewman noticed that the drinking water smelt peculiar. He told First Zentralemaat Robert Marquardt, 'The drinking water stinks!', to which Marquardt replied, 'Now take it easy my boy. We all stink here!'

112

But the man was not mistaken, there was a strong putrid odour to the water, both they and the water did indeed stink. The reason for their smell was clear as there was no shower aboard, but the water's smell remained unexplained and so Höltring ordered the drinking water tank examined. There the startled crew found dead rats in their precious water supply. The Brest shipyard must have made a huge mistake. Their task had been to fill and seal the fresh water tank before departure for patrol. Was it sabotage or just a terrible error? The answer was purely conjectural at this stage, but drinking water needed to be rationed. Fortunately the boat was not far from its base and *U-604* was tied up in Brest again after only five days.

The boat's 1 WO Hans Jürgen Stahmer left *U-604* to attend commander's training school. He eventually sailed as commander of *U-354*, its first patrol into the Barent's Sea where the boat was found north-east of the North Cape by British warships HMS *Mermaid*, *Peacock*, *Loch Dunvegan* and *Keppel* and depth-charged out of existence with all fifty-one crewmen.

Since *U-604*'s Atlantic mission had been prematurely aborted, most of the unused provisions aboard the boat were not returned but instead distributed among the crew who left the boat with suitcases laden.[63] In successive groups they were able to have leave in Germany, returning to their families with more food than many had seen for some time back at the home front. Maschinenmaat (Second Zentralemaat) Fritz Wagenführ was even granted fourteen days' leave to get married and honeymoon before returning to Brest. Thus the men were able to enjoy free time without the knowledge of the disaster that had overtaken the U-boats within the Atlantic. By this time the war in the Atlantic had reached its turning point, if not yet its lowest ebb. Allied ASW defence had reached such refinement that U-boat after U-boat was posted missing. As it later transpired after analysis of U-boat losses, May 1943 saw the most boats never returning from sea and was subsequently known as 'Black May'. In total forty-one[64] U-boats were lost in May; forty-eight[65] departed port for the North Atlantic during that month, so then the frightening proportion of losses was 85.4 per cent. Of course, this is not a true figure as it does not take into account those boats already at sea, but nonetheless it is a bleak picture. In addition, further U-boats sailed for different operational areas outside of the North Atlantic and these are also not included in those figures of boats that put to sea.

Nonetheless, in light of the horrendous losses being suffered it was perhaps very lucky for *U-604* that it had been forced to abort and spend time languishing in the Brest repair pens. Even Grossadmiral Dönitz acknowledged that the level of losses to his U-boat service had forced him on 24 May 1943 to withdraw from the North Atlantic – the primary theatre of operations for his U-boats and indeed the virtual *raison d'être* for the use of submarines as raiders against transport vessels. Dönitz recorded his thoughts in the BdU war diary:[66]

> Now the situation in the North Atlantic has forced a temporary shifting of operations into areas less threatened by air cover. Such areas include: the Caribbean Sea, the area around Trinidad, the area before the Brazilian and West African coast . . . At the moment those boats in the North Atlantic – that is to say those that possess sufficient fuel – will operate against traffic between the USA and Gibraltar. Besides the North Atlantic cannot be completely abandoned by our boats. It is necessary to let individual boats take their chances so as to keep the enemy in the dark over our changed intentions . . . it is therefore intended to begin any convoy attacks only when conditions are particularly favourable, i.e., at the new moon . . . These decisions mean a temporary break with the past principles of submarine warfare. It is necessary, so as not to sustain pointless losses while operating with inferior weaponry; this could break the U-boat service. There is, however, still complete clarity regarding the fact that the principle combat area for U-boats is the North Atlantic, and that the fight must be taken up there again with all firmness and determination as soon as the necessary improved weapons are given to the U-boats . . . it is to be expected . . . that after equipping boats with *Vierlingen* [four-barrelled quick firing flak weaponry], i.e., starting from autumn, the fight can be taken up again within the North Atlantic. In the meantime it is essential that the temporary defensive measures that we adopt do not affect the morale of the troops adversely: to ensure this will require not only the personal efforts of the commander-in-chief of the Kriegsmarine but the full support of all commanders.[67]

Dönitz confessed his defeat openly, acknowledging that there would be a wait as the largely outmoded type VII U-boats received improvement before they could return to the North Atlantic. Heavier flak weaponry, acoustic torpedoes such as the T5 *Zaunkönig* that could home on the propeller noise generated by enemy destroyers and thus provide some defence against them, new passive radar detectors like *Wanz* and gear that could search the centimetric wavelengths were all either under development or ready for distribution to combat boats. In the meantime they would concentrate on less heavily defended areas such as the Caribbean and the coasts of America, Brazil and Africa. Thus the morale of the U-boat service remained largely unbroken.

Meanwhile *U-604* lay in the Brest shipyard. Work on the diesel was lengthy as the damage so severe and it would not be until the end of June that the boat was ready for its next patrol. While in repair other technical faults were also found. Together with the dead rats in the drinking water tank there was the very real suspicion of sabotage though nothing could be proven. In the words of Fritz Wagenführ:

> I suspected sabotage in Brest. For example, we also found welding wire in the ventilation system. Apparently somebody had just left it there.[68]

While in for repairs other work was also carried out. The 88 mm deck gun was removed and a larger platform constructed at the rear of the conning tower to accommodate increased flak weaponry as described by Dönitz as part of the general upgrading of the VIICs.

While *U-604* was worked on, the situation confronting the U-boat men was obviously difficult. The family of Georg Seitz, farmers from the Mannheim region, applied to have their son released from front-line service, something that was possible under Wehrmacht regulations should certain criteria be met, for example hardship at home. They received the following reply:

Commanding Admiral U-boats, (Personnel Bureau U-boats), B.Nr. 25242 PU7c

To Herr Wilhelm Seitz
Regarding your application for the return of your son, Funkmaat Georg Seitz, from active service, there are guidelines about the withdrawal of soldiers from combat units and I am afraid that they have not been met in this instance.

Therefore I must inform you that it would not be possible.
Heil Hitler!

Kapitänleutnant M.A.

Track chart for the fifth war patrol
Days at sea: 5

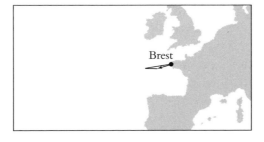

In fact during the course of my interviews with Herr Seitz it became apparent that he would have refused any such release from active duty in any event. He had his comrades that he would have felt that he was letting down if he had been transferred home.[69] In fact it was partly due to the enormous losses being suffered by the U-boat service in the Atlantic that there was such tight comradeship in the U-boat crews.

In *U-604*'s fifth war patrol and the period spent preparing for the sixth patrol the following U-boats were sunk by the Allies (22 April 1943–7 July 1943):

1	*U-189*	Kurrer †	sunk on	23.04.1943
3	*U-191*	Fiehn †	sunk on	23.04.1943
4	*U-710*	Carlowitz †	sunk on	24.04.1943
5	*U-203*	Kottmann	sunk on	25.04.1943
6	*U-174*	Grandfeld †	sunk on	27.04.1943
7	*U-332*	Hüttemann †	sunk on	29.04.1943
8	*U-227*	Kuntze †	sunk on	30.04.1943
9	*U-465*	Wolf †	sunk on	02.05.1943
10	*U-439*	Tippelskirch †	sunk on	04.05.1943
11	*U-659*	Stock †	sunk on	04.05.1943
12	*U-109*	Schramm †	sunk on	04.05.1943
13	*U-209*	Brodda †	sunk on	04.05.1943
14	*U-192*	Happe †	sunk on	05.05.1943
15	*U-638*	Staudinger †	sunk on	05.05.1943
16	*U-125*	Folkers †	sunk on	06.05.1943
17	*U-438*	Heinsohn †	sunk on	06.05.1943
18	*U-531*	Neckel †	sunk on	06.05.1943
19	*U-447*	Bothe †	sunk on	07.05.1943
20	*U-663*	Schmid †	sunk on	08.05.1943
21	*U-528*	Rabenau †	sunk on	11.05.1943
22	*U-186*	Hesemann †	sunk on	12.05.1943
23	*U-456*	Teichert †	sunk on	13.05.1943
24	*U-753*	Manstein †	sunk on	13.05.1943
25	*U-640*	Nagel †	sunk on	14.05.1943
26	*U-89*	Lohmann †	sunk on	14.05.1943
27	*U-176*	Dierksen †	sunk on	15.05.1943
28	*U-266*	Jessen †	sunk on	15.05.1943
29	*U-463*	Wolfbauer †	sunk on	16.05.1943
30	*U-182*	Clausen †	sunk on	16.05.1943

31	U-128	Steinert	sunk on	17.05.1943
32	U-646	Wulff †	sunk on	17.05.1943
33	U-657	Göllnitz †	sunk on	17.05.1943
34	U-954	Loewe †	sunk on	19.05.1943
35	U-273	Rossmann †	sunk on	19.05.1943
36	U-381	Pückler †	sunk on	19.05.1943
37	U-258	Koch †	sunk on	20.05.1943
38	U-303	Heine †	sunk on	21.05.1943
39	U-569	Johannsen	sunk on	22.05.1943
40	U-752	Schröter †	sunk on	23.05.1943
41	U-414	Huth †	sunk on	25.05.1943
42	U-467	Kummer †	sunk on	25.05.1943
43	U-436	Siebicke †	sunk on	26.05.1943
44	U-304	Koch †	sunk on	28.05.1943
45	U-755	Göing †	sunk on	28.05.1943
46	U-440	Schwaff †	sunk on	31.05.1943
47	U-563	Borchardt †	sunk on	31.05.1943
48	U-418	Lange †	sunk on	01.06.1943
49	U-202	Poser	sunk on	02.06.1943
50	U-105	Nissen †	sunk on	02.06.1943
51	U-521	Bargsten	sunk on	02.06.1943
52	U-308	Mühlenpfort †	sunk on	04.06.1943
53	U-594	Mumm †	sunk on	04.06.1943
54	U-217	Reichenbach †	sunk on	05.06.1943
55	U-417	Schreiner †	sunk on	11.06.1943
56	U-118	Czygan †	sunk on	12.06.1943
57	U-334	Ehrich †	sunk on	14.06.1943
58	U-564	Fiedeler †	sunk on	14.06.1943
59	U-97	Trox †	sunk on	16.06.1943
60	U-388	Sues	sunk on	20.06.1943
61	U-119	Kameke †	sunk on	24.06.1943
62	U-194	Hesse †	sunk on	24.06.1943
63	U-200	Schonder †	sunk on	24.06.1943
64	U-449	Otto †	sunk on	24.06.1943
65	U-126	Kietz †	sunk on	03.07.1943
66	U-628	Hasenschar †	sunk on	03.07.1943
67	U-535	Ellmenrich †	sunk on	05.07.1943
68	U-951	Pressel	sunk on	07.07.1943

† Commander killed in the attack.

U-604 had operated with several boats from the list of casualties: With *U-203* on their second war patrol as part of the Streitaxt group; *U-569* during the third patrol as part of the Draufgänger group; with *U-332*, *U-628*, *U-303* and *U-753* during the battle with ON 166 on their fourth war patrol. *U-659* had accompanied *U-604* into harbour at the end of the latter's second patrol, *U-659* sunk after colliding with *U-439* off Cape Ortegal.

The Sixth War Patrol

During the time-span of the sixth war patrol almost all boats that sailed from France operated exclusively in the South Atlantic where it was hoped they stood greater chance of success and survival following their defeat and withdrawal from the North Atlantic. Before the primary focus could be resumed Dönitz continued to despatch his boats to the Caribbean, America, Brazil and the African coast.[70] But the apparent sense of security was deceptive. In May 1943 eight U-boats sailed for American waters. In June another twenty-three war patrols, including *U-604*, in July another thirteen and in August eight more. From these fifty-two boats, twenty-three would never return and another six were forced to abort their missions prematurely.[71] The loss rate had exceeded 50 per cent in the new operational area.

By the end of July four U-boat tankers and an auxiliary tanker had been sunk, causing great difficulties for long-range U-boat missions. To compensate for these sinkings Dönitz ordered several type IX and type X boats to act as refuelling points in the South Atlantic. These were crucial in order to keep the type VIICs in action, such extended missions being impossible without the ability to replenish diesel during such long distances. It could take boats between four and six weeks to reach the coast of the American continent.

Before departing on their sixth war patrol the entire crew of *U-604* was issued with tropical uniform. Although the men were not told of their destination they could make an educated guess after this. They were aware that rather than returning to the North Atlantic, they were obviously destined elsewhere, perhaps the equator or beyond. The defeat in the North Atlantic had become obvious. Although the horrendous losses were not officially published the many empty spaces within the U-boat bunkers spoke clearly to the men. The U-boat men lived under the constant threat that their next patrol would be their last, but they must sail at all costs. There was no alternative.

U-604 departed from Brest on 24 June at 09.00 hours escorted by three minesweepers. For this sixth journey *U-604* carried a war correspondent, Herbert Kühn, whose task it was to report his impressions of the U-boat war in words and pictures. For the crew such a passenger was often known as a '*Badegäste*', a 'spa visitor', whose primary function was not for combat service aboard the boat. Kühn, however, was a veteran of active service during World War I and frequently assisted wherever he could with the day-to-day running of *U-604*.

The boat sailed with its small convoy from Brest and turned south, its destination Bordeaux. Three days from port another U-boat was sighted in Grid square BF 5551 at 07.40 hours; *U-518*, a type IXC outbound from Lorient. The larger boat joined *U-604* and the small flotilla continued on its southerly course hugging the French Atlantic coast, attempting to use the coastline and its myriad offshore reefs to disturb enemy airborne radar as much as possible. Their immediate destination was Cape Finisterre on the north-western tip of Spain from where they would sail into the open Atlantic. Höltring was optimistic about this new route, as they would successfully reach their target area by this method rather than by trespassing into the perilous Bay of Biscay. This course was known to the U-boat men as the 'Piening Route', named after the captain of *U-155*, Adolf Piening, who had first used it. However there was perhaps a slightly ominous note in the fact that Finisterre means 'end of the world'.

The constant air attacks on U-boats had brought about a change in German strategy. The boats were to leave only in groups where their combined increased flak weaponry could be used. The order continued that wherever possible they were to remain surfaced and fight the enemy aircraft rather than attempt to submerge; the period between the gun crew leaving their weapons and the boat being actually underwater was the point when the U-boat was most vulnerable.

So *U-604* and *U-518* continued as according to orders. Both U-boats completed the Piening Route without air attack, and were able then to steer west directly into the Atlantic. However, on 27 June at 12.37 hours as both boats surfaced a Sunderland aircraft from RAF 201 Squadron found them and attacked in grid square BE 98, 300 kilometres west of Cape Finisterre. The seaplane attacked with both cannon fire and four bombs. *U-604* was lucky – despite the standing orders to stay together and fight it out, Höltring ordered a crash-dive.

U-518, however, was slower and was hit and severely damaged. The boat was forced to break off and head home to the closest French U-boat base, which was Bordeaux. The boat suffered a further attack on 30 June at 11.05 hours from another Sunderland, this time from RAF 10 Squadron, but the six bombs dropped failed to inflict significant damage on the boat. *U-518* successfully reached Bordeaux on 3 July.

Presumably *U-518* had been unable to submerge quickly enough during the first attack, the larger boat being much more difficult to handle in such situations than the more nimble type VIIC. The time it took to get a type IXC under water amounted to some thirty-five seconds in ideal conditions, against the twenty-five to thirty seconds of a type VIIC. This was primarily due to the large surface area of the upper casing that had to be forced through the plane of the water's surface. Although this difference in diving time appears minor, when one considers that the attacking enemy aircraft could travel at an estimated 480 kph then every second spent above the water's surface, with no possibility of returning fire as the boat attempted to submerge, could be fatal. Presumably, therefore, *U-518* had been pinned to the surface.

Eventually Dönitz's 'stand and fight' order was cancelled. Only two U-boats from the entire fleet were exempt, the so-called flak traps. These boats were equipped with extra flak weaponry with the express purpose of luring enemy aircraft closer and hitting them with an unexpectedly heavy flak barrage. However, the Allies changed their tactics accordingly: upon sighting enemy U-boats the aircraft would circle out of range of the German weapons and call for reinforcement. Should the U-boat attempt to submerge then that was the moment to attack, when the guns were unmanned, otherwise the aircraft would attempt to summon surface units to deal with the U-boat. Thus the risk to the Allied aircraft was decreased and that to the U-boat maximised dramatically.

U-604 was scheduled to make a rendezvous with one of the few remaining type XIV U-boats at noon on 8 July south of the Azores in grid square DF 68. From this boat, *U-487*, *U-604* was scheduled to take on food and fuel. The radio men aboard both boats even planned to swap the records that they had. Aboard combat boats it was always a welcome change to have new music to listen to during the monotony of cruising towards action. It was the radio man's job to play music on the boat's gramophone, piped to all compartments over the communication system.[72] The rendezvous was successful and *U-604* able to continue on its path towards the South Atlantic, with additional fuel and supplies and fresh music playing aboard.

At this time *U-487* was the sole operational type XIV supply boat within the Atlantic. On that day there were only six examples of this type left. Three lay in French shipyards, one had been forced to abort its mission and a fifth was empty and returning.[73] However, on 13 July *U-487* was found and sunk.

An Avenger aircraft, flown by Robert P. Williams, and a Wildcat, flown by Earl H. Steiger, had both originated from the aircraft carrier USS *Core*. They sighted the supply U-boat and attacked, the Avenger dropping four Torpex depth-charges on the exact spot where the U-boat attempted to crash-dive.

Other aircraft from USS *Core* arrived on the scene and the depth-charging

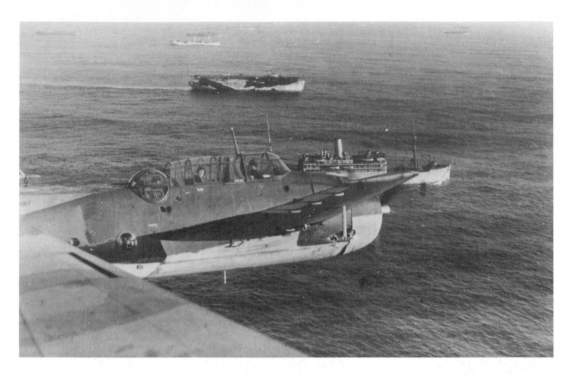

An Avenger aircraft, the same type that destroyed *U-487*.
(With kind permission of the Bibliothek für Zeitgeschichte)

sank *U-487* bow first. The flush deck destroyer USS *Baker* from the *Core*'s escort soon arrived on the scene and rescued thirty-three men from the U-boat's crew, twenty-seven killed in the sinking including the commander, Oberleutnant Helmut Metz.[74]

U-604 was soon included in a large patrol line near the Brazilian coast. Also included were the other type VIICs *U-598*, *U-591*, and *U-662*. The operational area for this straggling line was huge, spanning 1,000,000 km² of ocean – an extremely large area for just a handful of U-boats. Somewhat dramatically, from this handful of boats, not one would return from this patrol.[75]

The route to be travelled to the Brazilian coast was so distant that even though refuelled by the supply U-boat, most type VIICs would travel for days on only one diesel so as to conserve fuel. The days became longer and longer and as the boat approached the equator the interior temperature rose to a torturing 40° C. Only during the periods when the boat submerged into the relatively cool deeper water was there any respite for the crew and life made more bearable.

All four boats were making their first journeys towards the Brazilian coast and so far without incident. However, the first of them fell to enemy defences on 21

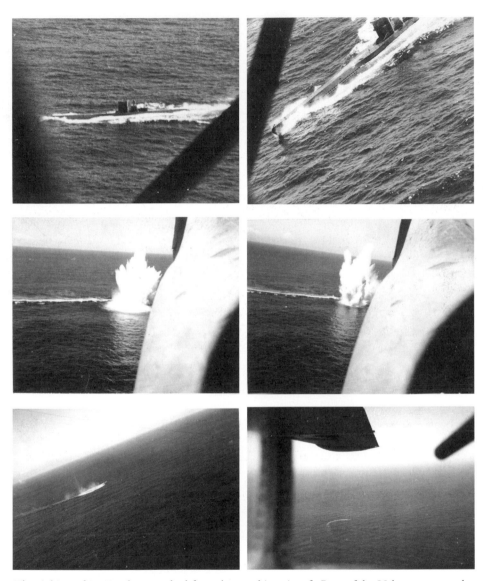

The sinking of *U-662*, photographed from the attacking aircraft. Parts of the U-boat crew can be seen manning their flak weapons. (With kind permission of the National Archives & Records Administration N-80G-85238, 85240, 85229, 85230, 85231 and 85235)

July 1943 when *U-662* was attacked by aircraft and sunk. In fact, *U-662* had first been attacked on 19 July by B-24 and B-18 aircraft and successfully repelled them with fierce flak defence. In the end it was a Catalina of VP-94 Squadron that destroyed the boat.

Crewmen from *U-662* photographed by the circling aircraft aboard their small life raft. (With kind permission of the USAF Historical Research Ageny USAFHRC-3814-581-16)

After the boat sank, a lifeboat was sighted by the aircraft. Five men had survived the sinking, including the captain, Heinz-Eberhard Müller, who had personally taken control of a flak weapon after strafing from the Catalina had killed the entire gun crew. Wounded, he was thrown into the water by the blast of exploding depth-charges. One of the German survivors died in the water and Müller and the three remaining survivors entered a pair of floating life rafts. After sixteen days adrift, circled by sharks, the four survivors were rescued by USS *Siren* after being found by a patrolling B-24. Another of the survivors died aboard the American vessel.[76] Their discovery was sheer chance – the majority of men from sunken U-boats left swimming in the Atlantic were never seen again.

On 22 July 1943 at 18.53 hours at 46° W, *U-604* passed the equator while submerged. Heat and humidity had made surface travel unbearable. After a message from BdU that the traditional 'equator baptism' was a very serious undertaking and should be particularly severe, Höltring, with the help of another crew

A Catalina flying boat. (With kind permission of the Bibliothek für Zeitgeschichte)

A certificate from the equator ceremony aboard *U-604*.

member, disguised himself as King Neptune to conduct the 'crossing the line' ceremony. For those already baptised on previous voyages it was great entertainment . . . for the newly baptised less so.[77] A former member of the crew of *U-604* later recorded the ceremony:

Equator ceremony aboard *U-604* on 19 June 1943 [actually 22 July 1943]. The commander Kaptlt Höltring dressed in an improvised uniform with another crewman as Neptune – King of the Seas – and baptised each member of the crew that needed it with seawater. They were then made to eat a pill with mustard, marmalade, pepper, curry and lots of other spices. Finally they were made to lie on a suspended tarpaulin where they were bounced into the air. Following this they were allowed a glass of schnapps and presented with a certificate showing their name and service grade. The entire ceremony was done under water at a depth of 40 metres.

One day after their celebration of passing the equator, a second boat from the Brazilian group was lost: *U-598* fell to air attack. Only two men survived.

On 30 July 1943 at 14.00 hours *U-604* was only 200 kilometres from the Brazilian coast, travelling surfaced. Radar and guns were unmanned, the propaganda reporter on the bridge alongside the lookouts making the most of the fine

Bridge watch aboard the conning tower.

weather to take photographs and film the boat at sea.

The boat's first watch officer, Oberleutnant zur See Aschmann, Bootsmaat Lurz and two other men were on bridge watch and would later report the series of events.[78]

The idyll would not last for long. A Ventura bomber from VB-129 approached from the sector 0–90° covered by Aschmann. It was flown by Lieutenant Commander Thomas D. Davies, USN, originally tasked as part of the airborne escort for convoy TJ2 headed from Trinidad to Rio de Janiero. Davies and his crew sighted *U-604* and they approached using cloud formations as cover, hitting a speed of 490 kph during the attack. The bridge watch were completely taken by surprise as the Ventura roared from cloud cover, spotting the threat far too late to prevent the attack. Davies flew overhead strafing the bridge with his heavy 50 mm cannons in the nose and following that with four Mk 47 depth-charges.[79]

With this first attack both Lurz and Aschmann were severely wounded; the former hit in the stomach and the latter having half his jawbone shot away and his carotid artery severed. Höltring immediately raced to the bridge and was also wounded, hit by shrapnel from the tower casing in both the left shoulder and his chest. The wounded men were hustled down into the control room and the boat put into a crash-dive. Then they were carried to the officer's mess, Lurz with his stomach wound laid out on the captain's bunk. Responsibility for first aid aboard the boat was the domain of Georg Seitz, who was wholly unprepared for such serious injury. He dressed the wounds as best he could.

Radio men aboard the U-boats were also the onboard medic in the absence of qualified medical personnel (carried on a minority of boats). The practical reason for this was that they were the sole members of the crew who were likely to have clean hands, required for sending coherent Morse and for writing incoming messages in the radio log.[80]

Aboard the Ventura, the pilot was of the opinion that the reduction in *U-604*'s speed was in preparation for a crash-dive. The boat had covered 100 metres from the spot of the first attack, and a depth-charge appeared to have landed between the conning tower and the boat's stern where it exploded violently. A 60-metre-high waterspout marked the explosion as *U-604* only slowly began to submerge and re-emerge several times as it turned 90° to starboard, after which it suddenly disappeared with three large air bubbles and an oil slick. The Ventura flew in for another attack; the U-boat's stern again slowly rising from the water so that the rudders and propellers were clearly visible. The boat stayed in this condition for nearly three minutes according to Davies's statement before sliding underwater with only a stationary oil slick to mark the boat's position, still visible after fifteen minutes.[81]

The PV1 Ventura that Davies flew belonged to the American Fleet Air Wing (FAW 16) and flew as part of VB-129 Squadron. The FAW 16 had been transferred to Brazil after the latter's entry into the war, the Americans able to station squadrons ashore on the Brazilian mainland. Davies's Ventura first arrived there in the middle of June 1943, stationed at Bahia. On 30 July 1943 he had begun his flight at 12.37 hours from his new home airfield bound for the convoy escort duty and sealing *U-604*'s fate.[82]

Aboard the diving *U-604* there were dramatic scenes. Aschmann had lost so much blood from his wounds that within twenty minutes he was dead. Rather than have the crewmen seeing the man's hideous wounds, his body was placed inside a hammock in preparation for burial at sea. Bootsmaat Lurz survived for two and a half hours after the attack before also succumbing to fatal wounds.[83]

The dive that *U-604* was on was not planned, and once the boat was off the surface she sank like a stone. Many of the crew were terrified as the depth gauge showed them their peril – passing the 200 metre mark. The hull began to creak frighteningly under the extreme water pressure. Only the luminous colour of the interior was visible, the pressure hull slowly deforming as the pressure increased. Chief Engineer Jürgens seemed frozen in terror and unable to issue orders that could save the boat. First Zentralemaat Robert Marquardt clenched his fists and repeatedly used all his strength to try to blow tanks and arrest their dive, finally bringing the boat's slide into the depths to a halt. The boat – rated by the shipyard to 90 metres – had reached a depth of 257 metres. Here once again was proof for the crew that Blohm & Voss made the best U-boats.[84]

Aboard the submerged boat the temperature was still about 35°. Surfacing was impossible in their present condition and so the air in the boat became steadily worse. The crew tried to mask the growing stench by pouring their 'Kolibri' aftershave on the floor plates in both the control room and the accommodation areas, but this only helped a little. *U-604* must surface within the next day to

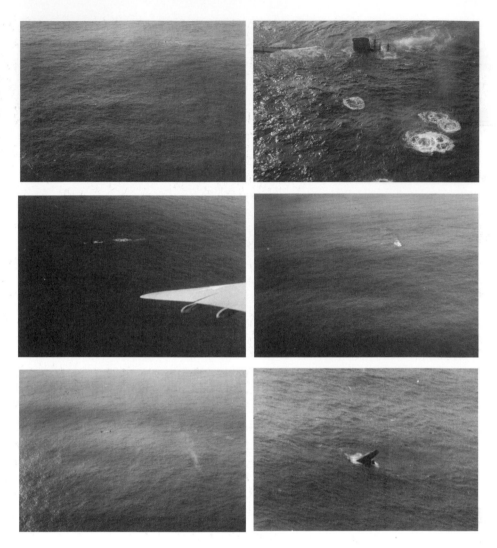

U-604 on 30 July 1943, 180 km south of the Brazilian coast when the Ventura piloted by Thomas D. Davies attacked; she is photographed from the attacking aircraft. At the top left, *U-604* can be seen at the top right. The damaged boat is still moving, escaping air creating a strong white wake as shown at centre right. (With kind permission of the National Archives & Records Administration N-80G-80564, 80586, 80581, 80598, 80599 and 80565)

replenish its air supply and to bury the two fallen sailors at sea. The corpses were both wrapped in hammocks, but rigor mortis had already set in and the bodies had to have their knee joints broken to allow them to pass through the hatchway into the control room and in preparation for lifting through the conning tower hatch and on to the bridge.[85] After preparing the boat to surface, *U-604* was able to emerge from the depths into a rain squall that at least sheltered them from enemy aircraft. The boat covered what was considered a safe distance from the sight of its presumed sinking and as only minimal crew members were allowed above decks Höltring conducted a brief ceremony and prayer for the two dead men through the boat's public address system so that all crewmen could hear it. Then the two bodies were committed to the deep wrapped in their hammocks and weighted at the feet.

The technical damage aboard *U-604* was immense and the boat was in a perilous state. Höltring would need every ounce of skill to reach a French base intact. The damage was serious: the port motor had been knocked off its foundation and wrenched out of place, as had the diesel fuel gravity feed tank within the engine room; several compressed air tanks had been destroyed and the Junkers compressor had been torn free of its mounting and needed to be secured by chain. The propeller shaft was leaking and water had flooded into the bilges, 500 litres needing to be pumped out hourly. Both periscopes were bent and useless and the conning tower was fractured and leaking a finger-sized stream of water. The boat's left rudder was so badly damaged that the left propeller could not be used as the boat would run in circles, and several tanks had been punctured so that trim was difficult to maintain. The boat faced a difficult journey ahead.[86]

Höltring radioed BdU to inform them of the damage suffered by *U-604*; a meeting with *U-591* was arranged to provide Höltring with medical attention. *U-591* was, like *U-604*, a type VIIC. It had departed France on 26 June and had also replenished from the supply boat *U-487* and been part of the straggling line of boats that patrolled the Brazilian coast. However, unlike *U-604*, this U-boat carried a doctor. Therefore BdU decided that they were the logical boat to come to Höltring's assistance. But their requests for information from *U-591* went

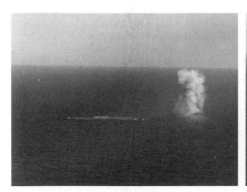

The sinking of *U-591* from the perspective of the attacking aircraft. The exploding depth-charge can be seen. (With kind permission of the USAF Historical Research Agency USAFHRC-3892)

The Natal base. (With kind permission from A.Wilson)

unanswered, since the boat was already lying at the bottom of the South Atlantic. In fact from the original group of four boats that operated together off Brazil, only Höltring's heavily damaged *U-604* remained.[87] *U-591* had been sunk the same day that Höltring had come under attack. The attacker was another Ventura, but this time from VB-127 Squadron stationed in Natal.[88] The pilot, Lieutenant Walter C. Young, had also been tasked as protection for convoy TJ2 when he had sighted and attacked *U-591*, sinking the boat 60 miles south of Pernambuco with twenty crewmen killed. Twenty-eight, including her skipper Kapitänleutnant Reimar Ziesmar, were later rescued.

As a second choice BdU contacted the type IXC/40 *U-185* and arranged a rendezvous with *U-604*. This larger boat, commanded by Kapitänleutnant August Maus, had departed Bordeaux, France, on 9 June 1943, also bound for hunting along the Brazilian coast. Like the ill-fated *U-591*, she also carried a doctor, Oberassistenzarzt Rammler. A point of comparison between the two types of U-boat to note is that *U-185* had been at sea fifteen days longer than *U-604* and without refuelling from *U-487*.

On 7 July Maus had intercepted a convoy before the Brazilian coast and sank three ships: the 7,061-ton *William Boyce*, 7,176-ton *Thomas Sinnickson* and the 7,176-ton *James Robertson*. He had also damaged a fourth, 6,840-ton *S. B. Hunt*.[89] His next success was at the beginning for August when Maus chanced upon the Brazilian freighter *Bage,* from convoy TJ2, and sank the 8,235-ton ship.

U-185 was some distance to the south when on 3 August the order came to meet *U-604* and during his dash to help Maus was attacked on 12 July south of Recife by a Catalina flying boat. However, the attack was successfully driven off with damage to the American aircraft.

Unfortunately the volume of radio traffic that was flowing between BdU and

U-604 and *U-185* for their planned meeting was providing the American listening stations with not only coded information but also the ability to track their positions with radio direction-finding. Höltring's messages were often lengthy: more than once Georg Seitz pleaded with his captain to shorten them but to no avail. As a result the Allies began an extended search for *U-604* and not just from the air; the American destroyers USS *Moffett* and *Jouett* also mobilised to find the boat. The two destroyers had successfully taken part in the sinking of *U-128* in conjunction with aircraft of VP-74 using the same search combination that was about to be employed once more.

With some indication of *U-604*'s location Lieutenant Commander Prueher took his Liberator belonging to VB-107 together with two others from his squadron and a pair of Venturas from VB-129 off the ground on 3 August to hunt and kill *U-604*.

Prueher took off at 05.10 hours from his home airfield at Recife and by 07.22 hours was over the presumed position of the stricken U-boat, 09°33' S, 30°37' W, which he promptly discovered and prepared to attack with his six Mark 47 Torpex depth-charges. He dropped them directly in the line that *U-604* took as it crash dived away from its attacker, the depth-charges hitting the water 16 seconds after the boat had submerged.

After the bombardment Prueher could still make out an oil slick on the water surface. Additionally, an underwater explosion was detected by the crew, but its cause remained unclear as once more *U-604* had been lucky. The boat sustained no significant damage and had succeeded in escaping with a last-minute crash-dive. Meanwhile the bomber crew sighted a second submarine, which lay 15 kilometres from *U-604* and immediately it too crash-dived into the depths. It can only have been *U-185*, though its identity remained unconfirmed. Prueher's Liberator circled for a further forty-five minutes over the area, in order to hold

The explosion of depth-charges from Lieutenant Commander. Prueher's aircraft on 3 August 1943 at 07.22 hours as *U-604* dived away. (With kind permission of the National Archives & Records Administration N-80G-84256)

The American destroyers USS *Moffett* (*top*) and *Jouett*.
(With kind permission of the Bibliothek für Zeitgeschichte)

the contact, but neither boat dared to surface. Afterwards the Liberator returned to Recife, in order to rearm at 10.20 hours with new depth-charges.[90] *U-604* stayed submerged, but that same day the American destroyer USS *Moffett* located the boat with ASDIC. *Moffett* dropped a depth-charge carpet around 20.37 hours, consisting of seven depth-charges, on the assumed position of *U-604*, a second carpet at 21.39 hours and five further depth-charges at 21.50 hours. Only in the early morning, at 04.08 hours did Höltring dare to surface and attempt to escape under the curtain of darkness. But USS *Moffett* was ready; she immediately gained contact and proceeded to open fire with artillery on *U-604*. Höltring ordered Aphrodite released to attempt to confuse enemy radar, in this instance successfully as *Moffett* and accompanying aircraft chased the wrong target.[91] Aphrodite was the name given to a radar decoy: it consisted of a hydrogen balloon to which was attached a cord with a small wooden rack that acted as a flotation chamber. The cord also carried three strips of aluminium between rack and balloon that reflected enemy radar waves, giving the appearance of a surfaced U-boat. Höltring had in the meantime submerged and, with only faint traces of the destroyer's propellers audible through hydrophones, *U-604* surfaced once more to continue the planned rendezvous and to charge batteries. For this purpose one diesel was used to propel the boat, the second switched to the electric motor acting as a kind of generator rather than turning the prop shaft. The severe damage that *U-604* had suffered, including flooding into the bilges and battery compartments, meant a man had to test the concentration of acid and electrolyte levels within the battery cells and add whatever amount of distilled water was required. The only access was by lying flat on a small carriage and rolling under the floor plating across the top of the batteries. There was just enough room for one man to roll over to complete his task. This was an important procedure as it presented a clear picture of the batteries' condition.

The mental strain on the crew of *U-604* was acute and their morale became increasingly fragile as they were aware of how slim their chances of survival were growing. Meanwhile *U-185* had also come under attack by Prueher's Liberator that sighted the boat at 17.35 hours and machine-gunned and depth-charged her. However, Maus's boat returned fire and damaged one of the aircraft's engines forcing Prueher to break off and head for Recife where twenty-three bullet holes were found in the aircraft.[92] *U-185* had not escaped injury either, a crewman seriously wounded in the attack. BdU was informed and subsequently ordered a second boat in the area, the type IXC *U-172*, to join the rendezvous. *U-172* had left France on 29 May, and her commander Carl Emmermann was one of the U-boat service's most experienced and successful captains; he finished the war having sunk twenty-seven ships.

On 6 August USS *Moffett* again sighted a surfaced U-boat, which immediately dived to escape. This was probably *U-604* which was again rocked by three depth-charges, though *Moffett* had not gained certain ASDIC contact and lost the boat. That day BdU radioed further instructions to the three U-boats:

Höltring, Maus, Emmermann. Grid Square FK 3955. Höltring to report by short signal whether the boat's return journey is considered possible.

Höltring replied shortly afterward that *U-604* was too heavily damaged to be able to reach France and BdU radioed final instructions.

1 Höltring and Maus meet in Grid FK 3955, one waits for the other. After meeting, sail together to FL 1255 there Höltring to give Maus remaining fuel as well as half provisions aboard. Also transfer whatever important items of equipment are possible.
2 Emmermann tonight report by short signal arrival in the latter grid reference. Take remaining provisions aboard and distribute Höltring crew evenly between the two boats. Then sink *U-604*. After the sinking Maus to report 'Yes' and both boats begin return journey separately.
3 Further redistribution of Höltring crew intended among other boats.

Unable to resist an opportunity Maus sank another ship en route to the rendez-vous, the 7,133-ton British SS *Fort Halkert*, and in the days that followed the American bomber squadrons intensified their patrols of the area in which the three boats were congregating. Höltring noticed the increasing air cover and reported it to BdU. Simultaneously he requested a meeting place further to the east away from the coast in an attempt to move beyond the range of land-based aircraft. BdU agreed and a new rendezvous at FD 9555 was transmitted to all three boats. Finally on 11 August at 10.00 hours in the appointed grid square 1,600 kilometres east of Natal the boats met. Initially conditions were perfect with clear skies that would allow warning of enemy approach, although clouds were gathering on the horizon that worried some crewmen. Detection of enemy radar had become increasingly difficult as enemy aircrews only switched on their sets at the final moments of an attack and thus visual sighting was needed to thwart an ambush.

But they had met and the transfers began. Emmermann's war diary recorded:

Boat stands on meeting place, course 290 degrees. Two U-boats sighted. 280°, E–S exchange, *U-604* and *U-185*!

During the next few hours Höltring transferred provisions and equipment to *U-185*, but this exchange terminated an hour after Emmermann's arrival so that *U-172* could also take material onboard. The war diary of *U-172* recorded:

Line connection completed. Provisions and luggage transferred by rubber dinghy. Delivery to Maus already terminated as Höltring assumes search group nearby, as he had detected ASDIC yesterday.

Then calamity struck from among the gathering clouds. In the middle of preparations for scuttling *U-604* Prueher's Liberator bomber emerged after sighting the three surfaced boats and skilfully approaching the rendezvous using the cloud cover. The combination of Allied code-breaking, radio direction-finding and intuition had given away the German meeting and he attacked with four depth-charges, all guns blazing. However, the Germans' luck had not completely deserted them and as all three boats began moving in zigzags they returned fire with flak weaponry and repelled the Liberator bomber. Seizing his opportunity Emmermann decided to dive, but *U-185* and *U-604* remained surfaced and continued firing, hitting the determined American bomber and bringing it down into the sea with its entire crew dead.[93] They were:

Bertram J. Prueher, Lieutenant Commander
Grover C. Hannever, Lieutenant
Robert Tehan, Ensign
Howard C. Brandon, ACRM
Donald W. Gardner, ARM2c
Gordon G. Merrick, AOM1c
Joseph Mihalsky, S2c
Clyde A. Smith, ACMM
John R. Van Horn, AMM1c
Eugene L. Coupe, Ensign[94]

Emmermann described the attack on 11 August within his war diary with an entry timed at 20.04 hours:

Aircraft approaches from great height out of the clouds. Attacked at low altitude of 40 to 50 metres. Attack centred on two connected boats, six aerial bombs; four to port, one between the boats and one starboard of *U-604*. On board flak firing from 3.7 cm and machine guns, hits possible. Very strong shock waves, both boats disappear in water fountains. Bombs were approximately 15 to 20 metres from boats on both sides. Maximum diesel speed lost, hose connector torn loose. Masch. Ob. Gef. Schiemann behind 10.5 cm removing muzzle plug, hit in neck and heart and killed. Second attack approach from port front. Boat begins moving. Flight altitude of 20 m, two depth-charges five metres beside boat, detonating approximately 20 metres behind the stern. Returning fire. Boat moves forward as Matr. Ob. Gefr. Wagner hit in breast and arm and badly wounded, Matr. Ob. Gefr. Meißner lightly wounded in the eye by splinter fragments . . .

Heavy damage to boat. Rudder wedges at port 10°. All boats move at all possible speed in zigzags giving mutual flak support. Possible ramming position for *U-185* which does not know of my rudder failure. Both machine guns fail. Chief Engineer announces clear to dive. Alarm! Dive since aircraft obviously has no more bombs and I cannot render assistance to Höltring with my boat in this condition. Submerged to A+20. Restoring of damage. Gyroscope remains inoperative. Magnetic compass occasionally unclear. Several cells cracked. Course north by magnetic compass.

Aboard the submerged *U-172* there were dramatic scenes with the wounded men and technical problems. Wagner, seriously wounded, was placed in the officer's mess, his condition was critical. He had lost a great deal of blood and required continuous fluids to help prevent shock. But he was strong and the bullets had passed through the wound, so fortunately did not require removal; an operation though not impossible aboard the U-boat would certainly have been extremely difficult.[95]

Following the destruction of the attacking bomber, the crew from *U-604* began transferring to *U-185* as *U-172* remained submerged. At first nobody dared to swim between the two boats until Obermaschinenmaat Ernst Winter leapt in to the sea; eventually all but two were left aboard *U-604*.[96] Leitender Ingenieur Jürgens and Zentralemaat Marquardt stayed behind to prepare the scuttling. Höltring, and some equipment that needed to be kept dry, had been transferred via a lifeboat owing to the wounds he had suffered in the air attack. The containers for the boat's torpedo pistols were used as flotation by some men as they swam to apparent safety. Once the men were aboard *U-185* the explosive timers were set and the main sea cocks opened aboard *U-604*. The position of the scuttling charges were not well known among the crew, in effect only three men aware of their position. The first one was in the bow compartment between the torpedo tubes, the second abaft of the main trimming tank.[97] The last two men abandoned *U-604* and after eight minutes, as Jürgens was pulled aboard *U-185*, the charges exploded and the boat sank, stern first, at position 04° 30' S, 21° 20' W.

Aboard *U-185*, Maus moved with greater deliberation not least of all because there was now over twice the planned number of people aboard his boat, upsetting trim enormously. For this reason BdU organised a second rendezvous with *U-172* in order to divide the rescued crew as originally planned. Emmermann radioed:

> Surprised by heavy land-based aircraft with bombs and machine-gun fire. Masch. Ob. Gefr. Schiemann killed another man badly wounded. Heading north. Slight damage. Since then no more air threat. Only part of Höltring's gear aboard. Assume search group still in the area.

In turn at around 02.49 hours on 12 August Maus also radioed:

> Aircraft shot down and Höltring crew taken over.

The remarkable fact is that despite the presence of the enemy at the exact spot of the rendezvous BdU still remained oblivious to the possibility that the Allies could decode German Enigma traffic. It was noticeable that the boats were attacked precisely according to location data. But BdU refused to accept the fact that the Enigma had been compromised. They looked at all other possibilities for the presence of the enemy there and also, as an added nod to security, double-encoded the messages that followed.

Emmermann aboard *U-172* received the following at 02.52 hours:

> Emmermann with M-officer and Tarnqu. Rendezvous with Maus for 12, during the evening to the north. Recommend transferring half of 'Höltring' crew with all possible haste.

Using the expression 'M-Officer' indicates that the message was doubly coded. Only one officer – not on the radio team, but usually the 2 WO – was permitted to decode this. BdU had apparently erred on the side of caution after the previous meeting by the three U-boats. What could have happened if the initial instructions had been double-coded is of course conjectural. Perhaps the aircraft attack could have been prevented, since the Allies would have only had radio location to find the U-boats.

Nevertheless, the two boats headed for their new meeting place in grid square FD 2841, far into the open Atlantic on the latitude between Rio de Janeiro and Salvador. *U-172* reached the appointed area on 13 August at round 21.15 hours and waited there with engines stopped. *U-185* on the other hand arrived the next day

The meeting between *U-185* (Maus) in the distance and *U-172* (Emmermann, foreground) on 14 August 1943. Half of Höltring's crew are in the water and swimming towards Emmermann's boat.

Half of Höltring's crew in the water between *U-185* and *U-172*.

at 11.13 hours. The two officers communicated with megaphones – called 'whisper bags' in the U-boat service – and apparently Maus vented his feelings about Emmermann's having dived while both *U-185* and *U-604* had fought it out with Preuher's Liberator. Emmermann, however, explained the predicament that his boat was in that led to the unplanned dive before feelings between the two men could run too high. *U-172* took on board the originally planned twenty-two

Notice the empty containers for torpedo pistols used as additional flotation by Höltring's men.

men, five NCOs, two senior NCOs and two officers. The heavily wounded, including Höltring, aboard *U-185* were not transferred on the instructions of the onboard medical officer. It was not just tactical considerations that decided who should stay and who should go. Those that had a particularly good connection with Höltring stayed aboard *U-185*. Those transferring to *U-172* swam across since there were no lifeboats available, *U-185* travelling ahead and the men trailing back to *U-172* that followed in line stern. This time the transfer passed without incident.

At around 12.47 hours the personnel transfer was complete and the two boats took up cruising speed as they steered their own courses towards France. A daunting distance of over 5,500 kilometres lay before them. In order to ensure the lookouts' concentration, the two boats sailed just inside visual range of each other after Emmermann had tested its faulty compass in detail. On 16 August he received a message from BdU asking for confirmation by short signal that half of Höltring's crew had been recovered to which he immediately replied in the affirmative. On the following day the boat's war diary records that the Metox became non-functional, leaving only visual detection of any enemy threat. By this stage of the war BdU was convinced that Metox actually posed a threat to the U-boats as the Allies could home in on a weak radiation signal transmitted from the device. Several U-boats had been attacked without any Metox warning which led BdU to this conclusion. In actuality the Allies had developed airborne centimetric radar that could not be detected by Metox. The Allies were actually aware of the weak radiation generated from Metox, but did not need this as their own radar obtained firmer results.[98]

Emmermann's chief engineer calculated that there was insufficient fuel and provisions to cater for a safe return to France with the increased weight and number of men aboard the boat. Thus a meeting with the type IXD2 *U-847* was arranged in DF 8635; Maus was also instructed to head for the meeting and take on supplies. A third boat, the type VIIC *U-84* commanded by Heinz Uphoff, was also included, heading back from a patrol in the Gulf of Mexico. *U-847* was the final member of the Monsoon group that had departed Norway bound for the Indian Ocean. This group comprised eleven boats, though only four would safely reach their designated base at Penang.

Kuppisch had departed on 6 July 1943, forced to return after ramming an iceberg in the Denmark Strait. The damage was relatively severe and the boat delayed for repairs before resailing. While outbound *U-847* had its task changed from the Monsoon group to the role of auxiliary tanker as a last resort after the sinking of the remainder. Without its ability to refuel boats several U-boats would have been unable to return to France following Dönitz's forays into more distant waters.[99] However, *U-847* was then placed in the situation suffered by other tanker-boats; it attracted all the other boats in the region becoming a bait no Allied hunter-killer groups could resist.

A former member of *U-172*'s crew recalled conditions aboard the boat:

> A crew member came down with a 40° C fever and collapsed in shivering fits. There was blood in his stools. Dysentery had broken out and Emmermann was glad to have the twenty-three extra men from Höltring's crew aboard who could replace those too ill to serve.

It is clear that several crewmen developed fevers and were incapacitated. The symptoms suggested that dysentery had indeed broken out aboard *U-172*. In order to minimise infection of the still healthy crewmen, those that were ill were forbidden to use the toilets. In effect one of the two onboard toilets was out of use anyway as it served as a food store and therefore the infected crewmen had to use an improvised toilet in the bow room. This consisted of a barrel placed

The carrier *Core*. (With kind permission of the Bibliothek für Zeitgeschichte)

between the forward torpedo tubes. This barrel, overlooked and surrounded by men confined within the crew compartment stank, of course, and the conditions are difficult to imagine. The boat was also travelling largely submerged to avoid air attack, though the barrel still required occasional emptying. For this it was carried through the boat to the conning tower and tipped overboard whenever the boat ran surfaced. Conditions were gruelling in the extreme.

On 24 August at around 16.13 hours, lookouts aboard *U-172* sighted an aircraft to starboard and the boat crash dived to 50 metres immediately; the sound of an explosion was heard aboard the submerged boat, probably a torpedo or bomb. Immediately the crew thought of Maus and the men aboard *U-185* who were sailing not far away. It later transpired that they were correct.

Aircraft of the escort carrier USS *Core* had sighted *U-185* and attacked it in the position 27° N 37° 06' W. The *Core* was on its second voyage from Norfolk, Virginia, having sailed on 16 August. During its first voyage its aircraft had sunk *U-487*, *U-67* and *U-613*. This time, on 24 August two aircraft – one Wildcat and one Avenger – had sighted the U-boat and attacked from cloud cover. The Wildcat pilot, O'Neil, fired at the boat's bridge and inflicted wounds on the entire bridge watch. When Maus arrived on the conning tower, the watch officer attempted to say something to him but was too badly wounded to speak. Robert P. Williams, who flew the Avenger, dropped two depth-charges which were very well placed. The port diving tanks were heavily damaged, the pressure hull ruptured. Additionally the batteries were ruined. Maus shouted to his chief engineer asking whether the boat was diveable, to which the chilling reply was 'Everything destroyed. Battery chlorine!' (*Alles kaputt, Batterie Chlor!*). There was no alternative: Maus ordered the boat abandoned, all men to go on to the upper deck with life jackets.

The American flush-deck destroyer USS *Barker*.
(With kind permission of the Bibliothek für Zeitgeschichte)

Chlorine gas formed rapidly if seawater penetrated the batteries beneath the officer's compartment, which it had aboard *U-185*. With diesels still running the gas seeped into the engine room and several men died at their station while the remainder scrambled for the conning tower and fresh life-giving air. In the bow compartment two severely wounded members of *U-185*'s crew lay immobile in their bunks, helpless in the path of the lethal chlorine gas. They had not managed to escape and faced a slow painful death by suffocation. Apparently Höltring was seen entering the chaotic compartment with his service pistol. The two men pleaded for Höltring to shoot them rather than face the lingering certainty of death by gassing, which Höltring did. Then, choosing suicide rather than abandoning yet another boat, he turned his pistol on himself and shot himself in the head.

On the bridge, meanwhile, Maus watched his boat slowly sink by the stern. The air supply for blowing tanks had diminished and the boat's list increased. Air attacks continued as the escaping men gathered at the conning tower and in its shadow on deck. *U-185* was still underway as the survivors began to abandon ship. Maus did his best to keep the men together and at the same time he shouted warnings to those from *U-604*: 'We are all from the same boat! Under no circumstances say anything!'

Men continued to die in their life jackets from the effects of the chlorine gas as more aircraft arrived overhead, although their attacks ceased when it became obvious *U-185* was going down.[100] One aircraft signalled that assistance was on the way and a few hours later the destroyer USS *Barker* arrived and pulled thirty-six men from the water, including Maus. Some still suffered from the chlorine, while Maschinen Obergefreiter Horst Ehlert had been wounded in the leg.

Of the twenty-seven members of *U-185*'s crew that were rescued, Leitender

U-185 under air attack on 24 August 1943. (With kind permission of NARA N-80G-77195, 77197, 77196A and 77198)

Ingenieur Herbert Ackermann and Medical Officer Georg Rammler both died from the effects of chlorine poisoning. Mechaniker Maat Erdmann also died on 26 August from his severe wounds, and Mechanikermaat Anspach the following day, again due to the effects of the chlorine gas.

In the following description, one of the survivors of *U-604* recounts the sinking of his rescuer *U-185* and the events that followed in American captivity.

I write this on 24 August 1943. Our temporary boat, *U-185*, strives to reach its designated grid square (to meet with a supply boat) proceeding at

Left: August Maus, commander of *U-185*, on the runway aboard USS *Core*. You can see his 'survival package' in his hands. *Right*: On the flight deck of the *Core*. (With kind permission of the National Archives & Records Administration N-80G-77210 and 77206)

cruising speed. My station is in the electric motor room. It is shortly after 10 o'clock in the morning when some huge bomb hits out boat heavily and caused severe damage. The usual procedures were followed, the diesels still ran and the command 'machine guns out!' rang throughout the boat from the loudspeakers as we worked feverishly at our stations. We in the electric motor area believed that the damage was not so bad, but chlorine gas from flooded batteries seeped from the bulkhead separating the galley from the engine room. We also suddenly noticed the effect of the impact as the boat heeled to the port side. We put on our life jackets and escape gear. I ran to the diesel engine room and on to the control room to ask what to do as we ceased to receive instructions. I told my comrades that if I did not return immediately they should leave. Crying and suffocating comrades lay on the floor of the engine room. In the control room men pushed their way up the ladder to the hatch, struggling for air. At the tower hatch stood the Kapitänleutnant. On the bridge Maus helped everybody to get out. I am suddenly up on top. Most of the bridge watch had been killed and corpses were lying in the hatch. Several comrades were already there, gathered in the tower. Aircraft approached from starboard at low altitude firing all guns on our dying boat. Men fell, men were wounded.

The diesels left a dark smoke trail as the boat leaned heavily to port. The stern was almost underwater. After the latest air attack I went on to the stern deck and held on to the antenna wire as the boat travelled slowly forward. The propeller wash and the vortex of water pulled at my body and I held on with all my strength, but it finally failed and I could hold on no longer. I left myself to fate and hoped that the propeller wash would let me go. My body

Left: Lieutenant Williams and Aviation Radio Man (First Class) Grinstead, who sighted *U-185*. *Right:* Capt. Wendell G. Switzer, Commanding Officer of USS *Core*, presents an Air Medal and the Distinguished Flying Cross to Lieutenant (Junior Grade) Martin G. O'Neil for his role in sinking *U-185*. (With kind permission of the National Archives & Records Administration N-80G-43138 and 364842)

left the boat and I was sucked underwater. After a brief moment I was at the surface once more, lifted up by my life jacket.

Before me I could still see smoke clouds and a small part of the bottom of the boat rose out of the water. More of my comrades jumped overboard and then the boat rose from the water and sank stern first; *U-185* our proud 'guest boat' lies forever at the bottom of the sea 400 miles southwest of the Azores.

I was still alone and looked for my comrades. Above me were four aircraft, whose size told me that an aircraft carrier must be nearby. A wave top lifted me and I spotted another man in the water. I swam toward him but he had no life jacket or escape gear. It was Schmiega from Upper Silesia from the crew of *U-185*. We both held on tightly to my life jacket and later found some boards that we grabbed hold of.

Some time later we discovered another comrade, who floated alone in the water, tossed back and forth by the waves. His head hung on his chest. We swam over to him and I lifted his head. His hair hung on his face but we could see that he had been shot in the head, in the middle of his forehead. I called him but no word ever came to his lips. We took the hard decision to strip him of his safety gear because Schmiega could survive. After we had taken it from him, our dear comrade who gave his life for our people, sank before us into the depths. But the life of a living man came first – nobody can condemn this act.

After Schmiega had donned the gear we kept a lookout for other men that we could gather in a group. Again on a wave crest we saw a group

The delivery of the uninjured (left) and wounded (right) crew members of *U-185* and *U-604*. These were transferred by the American destroyer *Barker* to the escort carrier *Core* by means of a line-and-pulley system. (With kind permission of the National Archives & Records Administration N-80G- 77212 and 77203,)

approximately 800 metres from us. So we swam towards them together. Still the aeroplanes circled above us. The sun burned down on us, burning the exposed parts of our bodies. My hair stank from the seawater and I became badly nauseous. I had kicked off my canvas shoes and rolled up my shirt sleeves. With great difficulty and force of will we reached the group of our comrades who were still alive. Many were wounded, though the seawater seemed to have stopped much of the bleeding so we didn't know just how badly injured many were, everything happened so fast. Comrades were helping each other. Sharks came into view, and to try to protect the wounded men they were sandwiched between healthy comrades, though my comrades told me some were still victims of the sharks.

Still the aircraft circled around us. Suddenly a man yelled, 'It's flashing!' A radio leading seaman deciphered the signals and we received the message 'assistance is on the way'. Approximately five hours passed, until another man called: 'Mastheads in view.'

Obviously it could only have been a hostile ship as our own could not operate here any more. Ever closer they came until soon we recognised an American destroyer before us. It approached at high speed and stopped, lying broadside to us at approximately 100 metres. Kapitänleutnant Maus swam to the rescue ship and asked for boats to be lowered so that those men who were unable to climb nets could be hoisted from the water.

The destroyer nudged slowly closer and sailors stood at the railings to help us. A ship's boat was lowered and as soon as it hit the water a sailor with a machine gun immediately pulled away and began the rescue operation. In the midst of the shipwrecked men a sailor suddenly raised his machine gun and fired into the water. As I learned later, sharks were being fired at to attempt to drive them away. The ship's boat went from man to man and collected all of the survivors. I was one of the last three taken up. My comrades were happy in the ship's boat as the sailor headed for the destroyer.

With a few lines the boat was secured to the destroyer's starboard side and lifted from the water. A sailor helped us out. How did we feel? Well, that day we had been saved, and deep inside we thanked the crew and command that did that.

Topside I had to take everything off and a sailor gave me a blanket to replace my clothes. A German-speaking officer immediately took our particulars while in the meantime our wounded comrades were taken and accommodated on a different deck. We were kept in the aft. Here we were given a Red Cross package that contained the following:

One pair of civilian trousers,
One pair underwear,
One sweater
One pair white socks
One pair trainers
One toothbrush
One soap
One tube of toothpaste
One belt.

We changed immediately, while in the meantime the Americans brought us a meal, which we wanted badly. Some things were strange to us as every country has its customs and undoubtedly also the USA was no different.

NCOs and crewmen that had no serious injuries were accommodated on our deck. Our senior NCOs and officers were housed separately. Once again the German-speaking officer appeared and spoke to us. We needed to be cautious about how we behaved. After four hours we were told that the carrier would be with us in five to six hours and we should then stand by for transfer. For the time being we lay down in bunks and covered ourselves with two blankets. In the afternoon we reached the carrier which lay to port. We had to go on deck for transfer ship-to-ship by 'breeches buoy'. The wounded were the first to be handed over. The destroyer's mastheads reached approximately up to the level of the flight deck of USS *Core*, so large was the size difference between the two ships.

While the transfer of men was undertaken the destroyer took the oppor-

Left: Once on board, the German crew were treated very well by the Americans.
Above: Burial at sea. (With kind permission of the National Archives & Records Administration N-80G-77211 and 77204)

tunity to refuel by hose connection. The German crews were herded closely together on the flight deck where we were filmed and photographed.

Unwounded men were ferried over two at a time, everyone issued a life jacket before the attempt. Suddenly a howling noise erupted and the delivery of men was called off. Seven PoWs were again sent below decks aboard the destroyer. Everything was cleared for action and the destroyer rushed off with us to chase a U-boat contact. A sentry guarded us with a machine gun, chewing gum always in his mouth. In the evening alarm bells rung on board and the destroyer went to full speed. The screws ground and thrashing water was hurled into the air. The rudder worked furiously and indicated that we were manoeuvring. U-boat alarm . . . and we were in the stern area?

We could hear hasty steps and rattling as depth-charges were made ready for release. The hull trembled as the engines roared. Everything was dark, a night lighting system burning with dim blue light. At the bulkhead a different sentry sat, smoking a cigarette and with a long wooden club dangling from his left hand. The speed gradually decreased and normal course resumed. I fell asleep . . . the first night aboard a hostile destroyer.

It was around midnight when suddenly a dull thud shook us awake. Frightened, we all jumped up until the sentry waved at us, indicating that we should lie down once more. In the meantime it was clear to us that depth-charges were being dropped, the underwater explosions well known to us. What we had experienced so often underwater we were now able to experience on aboard a hostile destroyer. We slept, long and deep.

All of the previous events lay heavily on us and we all had to deal with it ourselves. On 25 August 1943 we were woken in the morning by a sentry. Two men at a time could go and wash. Topside another guard took us to the aft area . . . one went to wash then the other. The depth-charge installations had again been brought back to readiness. New depth-charges were used. We knew the terrible effect if these landed nearby. Now the barrels lay before us in the form of cut-off cylinders with a diameter of 50 cm and a length of 1 metre each. A negro stood nearby doing laundry, his large hands kneading the laundry as soap lather poured from his bucket. The morning air did me a lot of good. The sky was clear and the sun was already high in the sky. The sea moved easily and flying fish travelled through the clear sea air. Once our time on deck was over we slowly returned to our temporary apartment deck. Breakfast was brought to us and soon we were all full. The meal was very varied. Thus the days passed aboard the destroyer. We were allowed one hour on deck a day and the German-speaking officer came repeatedly to talk with us. He asked our names and where we were from . . . He told us he had studied in Freiburg and spent much time in Germany. We couldn't answer all of his questions. He also spoke about the war situation. We explained to him that we were prisoners of war and under no obligation to talk about anything military. He loved his homeland and we ours, and so our loyalty to Germany came first. He saw our point of view and we continued to talk about other things as the destroyer headed back toward the carrier where it resumed its escort duty.

We could see the carrier from the destroyer's upper deck and saw also another three destroyers. Aircraft circled above and on the fourth day we again prepared for transfer to the carrier. We packed whatever belongings we were allowed to keep and were taken to the upper deck where we were transferred by breeches buoy to the carrier which lay on the port side.

Once we were aboard we were received by an officer who led us to the starboard side where a physician looked us over. The dispensary was very modern and well equipped. We were examined closely, including scars and registration numbers. I indicated that I had escaped chlorine gas poisoning. After the examination our fingerprints were taken, we were measured and weighed and asked for service details. From here I had a cross-examination by a German-speaking officer. After supplying the usual personnel information the interrogation began. Name and address without a street name, that was all that I said. After about ten minutes I was dismissed and went back with my comrades. First we were taken through different compartments where sailors looked on surprised, until we descended a steep staircase and an MP sentry opened a large bulkhead. Before us were the rest of our comrades on camp beds.

There was a big hello and we were glad to be reunited. First we received the sad news that four men had died on board; in the meantime they had been solemnly buried at sea.

We were each given white bedlinen and a life jacket. Our new deck had a height of 2.30 metres, width of 5 metres and a length of 10 metres. At the bulkhead there was a sentry stationed day and a night. Here, in this deck, we lived until we reached Norfolk, Virginia, on 2 September. A man came each day, in order to converse with us. He also brought us cigarettes every now and then rosaries. In our discussions he explained us that we can earn a lot of money, if we worked well. We could even buy cars after the end of war or take the saved money with us home to Germany. Also he asked us about the educational establishments in Germany, but we could not really give him any information. The sentries constantly supplied us with beverages, even if it was Coca-Cola in coffee pots. We marched to our meals in single file and then afterwards into a recreation area. This served at the same time as sleep and sports area . . . Meals were served on metal sheets with six sections. The meal was generally good and plentiful . . . A guard led us to a deck below the flight deck and here we could get plenty of fresh air.

We determined our course by using the sun, and could tell that we were heading west towards the USA. Our path back to our quarters after each time in the open led us as follows to starboard: the dentist, crew quarters, engine room, radio room, guard room, middle provisions locker, kitchen and then we arrived at our accommodation. For washing and showering we were taken to the toilet past the aft laundry. The grinding of the propellers was particularly loud there and in conjunction with the machine noises, strange sounds were produced. Everywhere we went crewmen had to get out of the way until we had passed. We were also allowed to shave for the first time aboard the carrier, but had to return the old blade immediately after use. What was particularly remarkable aboard was the high level of cleanliness, all decks were spotless . . . much importance seemed attached to cleanliness.

When at our daily meal we saw a crewman with placards on chest and back running around with a club. His job was to ensure that nobody threw a cigarette stub overboard that could give away the carrier's presence. He was eventually replaced by another man on this punishment duty. And so our days passed aboard USS *Core* between 27 August and 2 September 1943.

On 2 September we entered the port of Norfolk, Virginia.

We were all taken together by a guard on deck into the hangar where we were reunited with our officers. Around us stood a large contingent of American officers, among them the pilot Williams who had dropped bombs on us. Once the carrier was safely docked we disembarked. I want to mention briefly that the port was full of ships of all kinds . . . two or three aircraft carriers, torpedo boats, destroyers, as well as smaller vessels of all kinds – a powerful force of combat vessels.

First our wounded and officers were taken away, then NCOs and crewmen, disembarking in alphabetical order. In front of the gangway there was a column of cars, an ambulance and buses. The gangway was surrounded by reporters and we passed before them and many soldiers and civilian onlookers, both men and women. On the aircraft carrier opposite the crew all stood on deck, the whole navy base seemed to be on its feet. As we left the wooden stairs a German-speaking officer asked us our names, ranks and state of health. I was still suffering from chlorine poisoning and so announced myself as ill. I was then instructed to go aboard a particular bus, where two sentries with clubs guarded us lightly wounded men. The badly wounded men were placed in an ambulance and officers put aboard a special car. Healthy men were distributed among the remaining vehicles. After everybody was in place the column started to move. The journey went straight through the Norfolk navy base. Everywhere there were small buildings, mainly corrugated iron but some stone buildings. Between bushes and shrubbery there were carefully maintained lawns. We passed through two large gates and after a trip that lasted half an hour arrived before the gate of a two-storey military hospital. Our column had divided on the way, the patients ended up at this hospital while the rest of the men went straight to a special camp in the midst of an American prison.

We were unloaded into the hospital and two young sisters assigned us beds. The main accommodation within the hospital was divided in half by a long corridor, to the left the rooms were occupied by other German prisoners, but they were unknown to us and were shut off to avoid communication. On the right the area was assigned to NCOs, crewmen assigned to the area next to us. We were in steel beds with springy mattresses and white linen, as well as each bed having a night table. Furthermore some games and bibles were there too. With me were the following comrades: Ob.St. Karl Oppermann, Masch.Obmt. Richard Hußner, Btmt. Karl Düppengießer, Btmt. Georg Willmann, Masch.Mt. Fritz Wagenführ, Masch.Mt. Gerhardt Hauptmann. Next door was Masch.Ob.Gfrt. Horst Ehlert with a heavy knee injury where he had been shot.

The next day we had our hearts and kidneys examined and were given medicines that we needed, which for me was for the effects of chlorine gas poisoning. The medical attention here was very good. Also, some civilians came and took our measurements and then returned later with some articles of clothing. A Red Cross sister also passed by quite often and gave the smokers cigarettes. We cleaned ourselves on the first day but after that medical personnel did it and they had to take our body temperature and pulse and write down the results. We were given magazines to read, like *LIFE* magazine and the *New York Times*. We could see from the window some young navy girls being drilled in the hospital courtyard. An officer had them in line, marching back and forth and changing formation. Also some political exchanges were very interesting with the Americans. By Christmas 1943 they wanted to be in Berlin. Fate would decide and history later be the judge.

If you put the female personnel under a microscope you would have the following to say: They did their duty and always helped in every way. All the women were officers, orderlies and personnel of lower rank were men and had to stand at their attention. Their lips and fingernails were as red as blood. As they crossed the wards on their rounds their pleasant perfumed smell filled the air.

On our fourth day we were interrogated separately. Ob.St. Karl Oppermann was first and I was the next in line, escorted by a sentry with a club into the interrogation room. Six strong-looking men, in both civilian clothes and uniform, were in the room smoking. A large strong man, who looked capable of uprooting trees with his bare hands, sat at a desk. Beside him was an interpreter. What is your name? Where are you from? Who was your commander etc., etc? My answers were as before. I kept to brief vague statements.

After a short exchange a captain shouted loudly at me from my right and I shouted loudly back. Suddenly four civilians stood and threatened me. I clasped my hands behind me to keep them still. But I did not let them intimidate me. Shortly afterward I was allowed to leave the interrogation room and was returned to my bed . . .

After five days three men were transferred to the interrogation centre Alexandria in Washington. I, with four others, was moved to the PoW compound in the midst of an American prison where my other comrades were already. Also, thirty other men from different U-boats from the South Atlantic were there. Food was plentiful here also. From there we could see the American prisoners and became acquainted with their bitter lot in life.

We could see convicts of all races, each with a large 'P' on their back, as they came for their meals. Their hands were either on their chests or over their heads as they went past to their barracks, their feet in chains with iron balls attached. The MPs followed with long wooden clubs and pistols. We spent one night in this compound.

From there Wagner and his comrades were moved to the US Army base at Fort Mead and onwards to the Prisoner of War camp in Springtown, Oklahoma, before ending up in the PoW Camp Papago Park, Arizona.

In the meantime the families of crewmen from *U-604* received the news that they were considered missing scarcely one month after the sinking of *U-185*. It was usual at that time that in the absence of hard evidence and confirmation of a loss BdU would wait for a certain length of time after a boat's presumed sinking before making the official loss report. Meanwhile BdU would continue to demand an up-to-date report from any boat presumed missing. If the boat continued to be unresponsive, a second demand would be sent after which if no reply was received in a given time-frame the boat would be declared possibly missing. All radio operators in the Atlantic that were tuned to the same wavelength could hear these requests and so were able to form a reasonably clear picture of the losses being suffered at sea. It should be emphasised that radio operators were instructed to send reports of air attacks to BdU, but in reality there was often insufficient time in which a message could be despatched.

Below is a transcript of a message sent to the wife of a crew member from *U-604* in which her husband is reported missing. The rather blunt tone of the letter is striking and rather depressing.[101]

Missing Notice 22 September 1943
The Chief of Service branch M42.961

Dear Frau Wagenführ,
It is my painful duty to have to tell you that your husband must be considered as missing. The U-boat on which he was stationed had to be abandoned and sunk after damage suffered by air attack. The crew was transferred in two groups to other U-boats. However, there are serious concerns about the boat that your husband was transferred aboard. After a certain time has elapsed it has become apparent that this boat will not return. For this reason U-boat command has the crew – also your husband's commander – listed as missing as of 30 August 1943.

In the course of U-boat combat where each boat generally fights alone we often do not know much about the circumstances of a boat's loss. The U-boat was, however, possibly sunk by aircraft. Nonetheless, there remains total uncertainty regarding the fate of the crew.

I know that now, dear Frau Wagenführ, you will face a terrible time of waiting and worrying. You can rest assured that from our side, everything humanly possible is being done to clarify the fate of our comrades. We are in constant contact with the Red Cross and military agencies who can help clarify what happened, and we are always the first to be informed. I would like to therefore ask that you trust us and try not to sadden yourself and think too much about the possible answers. As soon as we know anything we will let you know. Sometimes personal messages from enemy captivity actually come quicker than via official channels so I would also ask that you inform me immediately if you receive anything. Naturally you will hear any good news from us as soon as possible.

In the base whatever property belongs to your husband is being conscientiously collected by an officer and will be forwarded to you. For all questions of any kind, use only our military postal service number M42961. Of course, we shall assist you with advice and information as much as possible.

From the bottom of my heart I hope for good news for you soon.

Heil Hitler!
Yours sincerely,
The Undersigned
Lehmann-Willenbrock

Within five months the wife of crewman Maschinenmaat Fritz Wagenführ learnt that her husband was indeed alive and in American captivity, after which she received another personal message from the commander of the 9th U-Flotilla.[102]

Korvettenkapitän Lehmann-Willenbrock 7 February 1944
Chief of the Service branch M42.961

Dear Frau Wagenführ
I heartily congratulate you and confirm the letter dated 15 January 1944.

Heil Hitler!
Yours Sincerely
Lehmann Willenbrock

We can now return to 24 August 1943 and the day that *U-185* was sunk. On that same day an Avenger from the escort carrier sank Uphoff's *U-84*, which like *U-172* and *U-185* had been instructed to rendezvous with Kuppisch in *U-847* and take on extra fuel. *U-84* actually sighted the attacking aircraft and dived, but the Avenger was armed with a FIDO homing torpedo which it dropped above the dived boat. Since then the boat was considered missing by BdU. The FIDO was an American-developed acoustically guided weapon, similar in essence to the T5 Zaunkönig torpedo. It had a diameter of 48 centimetres and a length of 2.13 metres, weighing 308 kilograms. The warhead carried 41.7 kilograms of Torpex, the whole thing propelled by a 5-kilowatt electric motor supplied with a current of 110 amperes from a 48-volt lead-acid battery. The FIDO could cover 3,700 metres at a speed of 10 knots as it hunted for targets. The electric drive and guidance system had been developed by General Electric. The FIDO was launched by aircraft from a height of up to 90 metres as the plane travelled at no more than 220 kph. The FIDO continued in production after the war and altogether between March 1943 and 1949 4,000 torpedoes had been manufactured with a unit price of $1,800. 340 of them were fired at submarines and 37 boats were sunk, a further 18 heavily damaged.

Interestingly, pilots were only allowed to use the FIDO if they could guarantee that no other member of the Axis forces could observe the weapon being used. By this method the Allies managed to keep the secret of FIDO throughout World War II. If the Germans had become aware of it they could also have learned that if U-boats submerged with lower screw revolutions they could have escaped the acoustic sensors, which at that stage could only follow loud noises.

Meanwhile Emmermann continued under water and emerged only at around 23.06 hours on 24 August without knowing exactly what had happened to *U-185*, though the distant explosions had certainly left him with suspicions. *U-172* operated at cruising speed heading 340° in order to meet Kuppisch. On 25 August, one day after Maus's sinking, Emmermann saw the shadow on the horizon at 09.32 hours that signalled the rendezvous was made, *U-847* emerging into sight while supplying *U-508*.

Emmermann ordered lookouts doubled and all flak weapons manned. Only those men essential for the supply operation were allowed on deck, all others being ordered to remain below in order to decrease diving time in the event of attack. But Emmermann couldn't believe his eyes. He found Kuppisch and his crew carelessly scattered around *U-847*.

A member from Höltring's crew who was aboard *U-172* at the time remembered that Kuppisch and his men behaved as if they were on 'a Strength Through Joy steamer' on a peacetime lake.[103] Kuppisch had not been to sea for

The meeting on 25 August 1943 between *U-847* (left) and *U-172*. Kuppisch's boat was sunk three days later.

some time before this patrol and thus did not really understand the terrible danger posed by enemy aircraft as the enemy's defences and attack capabilities had changed greatly in the time he had been ashore. Kuppisch continued to believe that he was in the 'Air Gap' – that area of the central Atlantic where no hostile aircraft could reach. But this gap had long been closed, and the Allies were capable of searching the entire Atlantic for U-boat targets. Emmerman severely admonished Kuppisch, telling him that he should at least immediately man his flak weapons and keep the resupply time as brief as possible.

Emmermann did not transfer any of Höltring's crew to *U-508* as the dysentery had so weakened his crew that he needed every able-bodied man he could keep aboard his boat. Therefore no men were handed over during the resupply. However, *U-508* continued to wait in the area for *U-185* in order to perhaps relieve the burden of extra men carried aboard Maus's boat, unaware of course that *U-185* had already been sunk.

After the resupply was complete Emmermann set course for 45° and the sanctuary of France. Both *U-847* and *U-508* waited for Maus. Of the three original boats destined to meet *U-847*, only Emmermann succeeded as both *U-84* and *U-185* were destroyed. Three days later *U-847* was also sunk. Kuppisch announced by radio that the initial supply missions had been accomplished. This message was pinpointed by Allied Huff-Duff who immediately homed in on a hunter-

U-172 runs into Lorient on 7 September 1943 with half the crew of *U-604* aboard. In front on the left is Obergefreiter Wagner from the crew of *U-185* who had been shot in the chest during the attack on Maus's boat on 3 August.

killer group centred on the carrier USS *Card* to find and destroy. *Card* was the replacement carrier for USS *Core* which had in the meantime headed back to Norfolk. Within hours aircraft had found the meeting place designated by *U-847* and attacked. The aircraft came in with all guns blazing which Kuppisch's tardy flak could not hope to defeat. The boat was immediately ordered to dive, although this left the boat defenceless for vital seconds. As *U-847* started to submerge the attacking aircraft bore in again and this time dropped a FIDO on the path of the moving boat. The propellers were operating at maximum to drive the boat under and so gave the FIDO a perfect target. The boat was so shallow that attacking aircrew were able to follow it as it homed on its target, its path ending in a shattering underwater explosion.[104] The U-boat crew stood no chance and slid below to the 2,000 metre seabed.

Emmermann received a radio message on 30 August from *U-508* that not only had Maus failed to arrive, but *U-847* was also probably sunk. Emmermann pressed

The carrier *Card*. (With kind permission of the Bibliothek für Zeitgeschichte)

on regardless and followed the Piening Route towards its home port of Lorient. On 7 September *U-172* entered Lorient, its luck holding all the way home as the distinctive sound of an anchor chain from a suspended mine dropped by the RAF in the harbour approaches could be heard scraping along the U-boat's keel . . . but with no ensuing explosion.[105]

When running into Lorient even Matrose Obergefreiter Wagner from *U-185* who had been badly wounded in the arm and chest during the air attack on 11 August stood on deck. It was amazing how far Wagner had actually managed to recuperate from his wounds considering the conditions aboard Emmermann's boat during the voyage. After the welcoming ceremony Wagner was taken by ambulance to hospital where the bullet was removed from his chest.

Following Emmermann's successful return to Lorient he was presented with the Oak Leaves to his Knight's Cross that he had been awarded while still at sea, whereupon he departed combat U-boats and became the commander of the 6th U-Flotilla in Saint Nazaire. Emmermann's crew had painted the Oak Leaves on the conning tower of *U-172* and presented him with home-made versions while aboard the boat on patrol. Emmermann therefore handed over his boat to another commander, his erstwhile 1 WO Hermann Hoffman. At this time Emmermann had been responsible for sinking 180,000 BRT of enemy shipping. Likewise Maus was also awarded a medal, the Knight's Cross bestowed on him while in captivity for his part in the rescue of the crew of *U-604* once survivors had recounted the full story to their superiors. Two crewmen from *U-604* were similarly decorated; Leitender Ingenieur Jürgens and Zentralemaat Marquardt were both awarded the German Cross in Gold for their part in the success scuttling of Höltring's boat. Of the four boats that had been despatched by BdU to hunt off the Brazilian coast, none returned. Only half of Höltring's crew made it back to France aboard *U-172*. From the four boats 123 men lost their lives, 65 having survived. There had

Commander Emmermann (left), and the chief engineer of *U-604*, Helmut Jürgens, pictured as
U-172 ran into Lorient. Here can clearly be seen the camera that Jürgens is holding and that
certainly shot many of the pictures contained here.

been fewer ships sunk than U-boats. Such an exchange rate was untenable, yet it
was sustained almost until the war's end.

Statement from BdU regarding the war patrol of U-172

With proven energy and good fortune the undertaking was accomplished
which brought the boat a pleasing success. The lucky defence against several
aircraft is thanks to prudent and correct behaviour. Nothing else to note.

U-604 was on its sixth war patrol and forty-nine days at sea before it was sunk.
Following interviews with contemporary witnesses who were aboard *U-172* and
who experienced conditions aboard during the return voyage, it has become clear
that it was not in fact dysentery that affected the boat. Perhaps it was the shattered
nerves of the crew members that gave rise to fever and symptoms comparable
with those of dysentery. In any event, it was not necessary to hospitalise the men
from *U-172* thus affected after their return to France: real dysentery would have
required this as a standard course of action.

Emmermann handed over command to his 1 WO, Hermann Hoffman, who
had already established a good relationship with the crew having served as 1 WO
and 2 WO. Nonetheless, *U-172* was sunk during its next patrol by a combination

of air strikes and depth–charges on 13 December 1943 west of the Canary Islands. Forty-six crewmen survived, including Hoffmann; fourteen others died with the boat.

The Track Chart for the sixth war patrol
Note: This is an approximation of the sixth war patrol track chart: an exact reconstruction is impossible due to missing war diary entries.

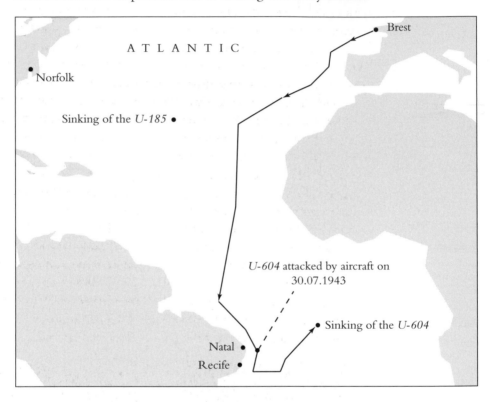

In the time span of *U-604*'s sixth war patrol and the period spent aboard *U-185* and *U-172* the following U-boats were sunk by the Allies (8 July–7 September 1943):

1	*U-232*	Ziehm	sunk on	08.07.1943
2	*U-514*	Auffermann	sunk on	08.07.1943
3	*U-435*	Strelow	sunk on	09.07.1943
4	*U-590*	Krüer	sunk on	09.07.1943
5	*U-409*	Massmann	sunk on	12.07.1943
6	*U-506*	Würdermann	sunk on	12.07.1943

7	*U-561*	Henning	sunk on	12.07.1943
8	*U-487*	Metz	sunk on	13.07.1943
9	*U-607*	Jeschonnek	sunk on	13.07.1943
10	*U-160*	Pommer †	sunk on	14.07.1943
11	*U-135*	Luther	sunk on	15.07.1943
12	*U-159*	Beckmann †	sunk on	15.07.1943
13	*U-509*	Witte †	sunk on	15.07.1943
14	*U-67*	Müller †	sunk on	16.07.1943
15	*U-513*	Guggenberger	sunk on	19.07.1943
16	*U-558*	Krech	sunk on	20.07.1943
17	*U-662*	Müller	sunk on	21.07.1943
18	*U-527*	Uhlig	sunk on	23.07.1943
19	*U-598*	Holtorf †	sunk on	23.07.1943
20	*U-613*	Köppe †	sunk on	23.07.1943
21	*U-459*	Wilamowitz †	sunk on	24.07.1943
22	*U-759*	Friederich †	sunk on	26.07.1943
23	*U-359*	Förster †	sunk on	28.07.1943
24	*U-404*	Schöneberg †	sunk on	28.07.1943
25	*U-614*	Sträter †	sunk on	29.07.1943
26	*U-43*	Schwanke †	sunk on	30.07.1943
27	*U-375*	Könekamp †	sunk on	30.70.1943
28	*U-461*	Stiebler	sunk on	30.07.1943
29	*U-462*	Vowe	sunk on	30.07.1943
30	*U-504*	Luis †	sunk on	30.07.1943
31	*U-591*	Ziesmer †	sunk on	30.07.1943
32	*U-199*	Krauss †	sunk on	31.07.1943
33	*U-383*	Kremser †	sunk on	01.08.1943
34	*U-454*	Hackländer	sunk on	01.08.1943
35	*U-106*	Damerow	sunk on	02.08.1943
36	*U-706*	Zitzewitz †	sunk on	03.08.1943
37	*U-572*	Kummetal †	sunk on	03.08.1943
38	*U-647*	Hertin †	sunk on	03.08.1943
39	*U-489*	Schmandt	sunk on	04.08.1943
40	*U-34*	Frenski	sunk on	05.08.1943
41	*U-117*	Neumann †	sunk on	07.08.1943
42	*U-615*	Kapitzky †	sunk on	07.08.1943
43	*U-664*	Gräf	sunk on	09.08.1943
44	*U-525*	Drewitz †	sunk on	11.08.1943
45	*U-468*	Schamong	sunk on	11.08.1943

46	*U-403*	Heine †	sunk on	17.08.1943
47	*U-197*	Bartels †	sunk on	20.08.1943
48	*U-458*	Diggins	sunk on	22.08.1943
49	*U-84*	Uphoff †	sunk on	24.08.1943
50	*U-134*	Brosin †	sunk on	24.08.1943
51	*U-185*	Maus	sunk on	24.08.1943
52	*U-523*	Pietsch	sunk on	25.08.1943
53	*U-847*	Kuppisch †	sunk on	27.08.1943
54	*U-634*	Dahlhaus †	sunk on	30.08.1943
55	*U-669*	Köhl †	sunk on	07.09.1943

† Commander killed in the sinking.

From the above casualty list some boats have been mentioned already as having operated with *U-604*. *U-468* and *U-454* were both with *U-604* during the fourth war patrol and action against ON 166. *U-409* was with Höltring in the Streitaxt Group during the second war patrol. The supply boat *U-462* from which Höltring received spare parts for the faulty Metox during the fourth patrol now also lay at the bottom of the Atlantic. Last of all, of course, were *U-874* and *U-185*.

The crew of U-604 after the sixth war patrol
With *U-172* (Emmerman) sailing into Lorient
  Helmut Jürgens (Oberleutnant. Ingenieur, Leitender Ingenieur)
  Herbert Kühn (Oberleutnant zur See der Reserve, P.K.)
  Albert Finster (Obersteuermann and 3 WO)
  Wilhelm Schiffer (Obermaschinist (Diesel))
  Peter Binnefeld (Oberbootsmaat seemann no. 2)
  Walter Ortwein (Maschinenmaat)
  Georg Seitz (Funkmaat)
  Marquardt Robert (First Zentralemaat)
  Heinrich Reiblich (Torpedo Mech Obergefreiter)
  Horst Gebauer (Matrose Obergefreiter)
  Peter Seipel (Maschinen Obergefreiter)
  Ernst Werner (Maschinen Obergefreiter)
  Erwin Klawien (Masch. Obergefreiter)
  Heinz Müller (Funkobergefreiter)
  Ewald Anschütz (Torp. Mech. Gefreiter)
  Werner Beher (Matrose Obergefreiter)
  Eduard Rogowski (Matrose Obergefreiter)
  GünterAlrutz (Matrose Obergefreiter)

Otto Schreckenbach (Maschinen Obergefreiter)

Ernst Schröter (Maschinen Obergefreiter)

Hans Beck (Maschinen Obergefreiter)

Fred Fröde (Maschinenmaat (Diesel))

Hugo Schuhmacher (Maschinen Obergefreiter)

Fallen crew members

Horst Höltring (Kommandant)

Frank Aschmann (1 WO officer and Oberleutnant zur See)

Herbert Lurz (Bootsmaat Seemann no. 3)

Gerhard Beugholz (Obermaschinist)

Helmut Altmann (Oberbootsmaat seemann No. 1)

Ernst Schnede (Torpedo Mech. Maat)

Adolf Helsper (Obermaschinenmaat (Diesel))

Horst Keller (Funkmaat)

Richard Opitz (Matrose Obergefreiter)

Werner Schulz (Matrose Obergefreiter)

Ferdinand Bibo (Matrose Obergefreiter (cook))

Rudolf Rotthner (Maschinen Obergefreiter)

Karl Strauch (Maschinen Hauptgefreiter)

Walter Lux (Funkobergefreiter)

Bellmann Paul (Torpedo Mech. Gefreiter)

Wilhelm Schnitte (Matrose Gefreiter)

After the sinking of *U-185*, the crew members held in American captivity.

Fritz Wagenführ (Maschinenmaat (second Zentralemaat))

Ernst Winter (Obermaschinenmaat (E-Maschine))

Heinz Trommer (Maschinen Obergefreiter)

Horst Ehlert (Maschinen Obergefreiter)

Werner Eismann (Matrose Gefreiter)

Heinz Lüttges (Maschinen Obergefreiter)

Gerhard Krimmling (Maschinen Gefreiter)

Dr v. Bothmer (2 WO and Oberleutnant zur See)

Walter Nieswand (Torpedo Mech. Obergefreiter)

The Return Home from the Sixth War Patrol

After they had run into Lorient aboard Emmermann's *U-172*, covering 3,588 nautical miles aboard the boat, the survivors from *U-604* were fetched a day later by bus and taken north to Brest. There the crew recovered their belongings that had been stored during the mission. Much to many men's annoyance some belongings had been misplaced.[106]

Those that had been aboard *U-185* and either been killed or captured had had their personal effects sent to their families.

After a short stay in Brest the remainder of Höltring's crew were sent to the submarine convalescent home Bad Wiessee at Tegernsee in Bavaria. This was a necessary procedure for the crew whose nerves were severely frayed by events during their last patrol. Zentralemaat Robert Marquardt, for example, did not manage to recover his nerves even while staying ashore. As he slept in a room in

Roll call of the remainder of *U-604*'s crew in the headquarters of the 9th U-Flotilla, today used as the hospital that it was planned to be. The bunker in the background is still standing.

the convalescence centre a bell rang in the adjoining room and he leapt from his bed and began looking for the exhaust vents to close in order to dive the boat.[107] The majority of the crew were in the same mental condition. Thus the stay at the home was primarily for recovery and not jolly events. Bad Wiessee was not the only such convalescence home for the U-boat service, there were others in Weissach, Weilersbach and, of course, France, such as the Chateau Trevarez. These homes were rather well hyped by the U-boat service as well, as this excerpt from an advertising article on one such home shows. It is also interesting to see how the effect of the growing air strikes on Germany is described openly.

Lines are thrown over hawsers, the boat firmly laid against the jetty of the home port. After long weeks the crew finally gets firm land under their feet again. And not only that, they also get: vacation passes! Many days of peace in which to unwind and regain their strength for new tasks ahead.

But, of course, many men ask themselves 'where can we go on vacation?' to which no one has an answer. One has had his home smashed in the Allied terror bombing; another has moved his family away to less endangered areas and so they are in a different place from the one that he knows as his old homeland. And now in such disadvantaged situations the Commanding Admiral of the U-boat service has taken the opportunity to give the men their heart's desires to unwind in quiet, alarm-free, beautiful areas of Germany in convalescent homes they created, gates open wide to our holiday-makers all year round.

Above: Photograph taken outside the U-boat convalescent home in Bad Wiessee.
Right: From left to right: Funkmaat Georg Seitz, Masch.-Gefr. Ernst Schröter and Masch.-Gefr. Otto Schreckenbach in the U-boat convalescent home in Bad Wiessee. In the background can be seen a sign that reads '*Erholungsheim der U-Bootwaffe*'.

The New Boat U-873

A fter three weeks in the U-boat convalescent home in Bad Wiessee, the entire remnant of *U-604*'s crew was transferred to Bremen for the familiarisation process ('*Baubelehrung*') for *U-873*. So they began everything once again with a new boat.

Maschinenmaat Fred Fröde, after all of the strain suffered from his experiences aboard *U-604*, was classified as unfit for U-boat service and dismissed. First Zentralemaat Robert Marquardt became the trainer at the AG Weser shipyard in Bremen.[108] He had the task of teaching about the technical aspects of a U-boat at the Kriegschiffbau-Lehranstalt (Sixth Warship-building School). Other former crew members from *U-604* were transferred to NCO training so that only a fraction of Höltring's crew remained to take part in the familiarisation process that accompanied the construction of *U-873*.

However, it is only with the brief history of *U-873* that the history of *U-604* and its crew finally ends and can be fully understood. Thus I would like to add the following brief outline of the history of *U-873*. Additionally, even without the connection to *U-604*'s crew, the history of *U-873* is as interesting as it is mysterious, and indeed would soon become infamous.

The commander of the new boat *U-873*, Friedrich Steinhoff, was born in Thüringen in 1909 and entered the German navy in 1934. Before he began his military career Steinhoff had a career within the merchant navy as an officer and master. His first military command began with the commissioning of *U-511* on 8 December 1941. He commanded this boat until 12 December 1942. After commissioning, this type IXC boat was seconded to the UAG, UAK and Agru Front as a test-bed for experimental purposes.

The boat was attached to the rocket laboratory in Peenemünde between 31 May 1942 and 5 June 1942 to be used as a mobile firing platform for rocket projectiles. It was the first attempt at firing rockets from a submerged U-boat in what was code-named 'Project Ursel'. The choice of Friedrich Steinhoff and *U-*

511 for the experiments was not accidental – his brother, Dr Eric Steinhoff, was part of Peenemünde's rocket development team. Thus the two brothers worked in close collaboration in the trials. It is also interesting to note that at the war's end, when Eric Steinhoff was captured, he and other scientists were immediately transported to the USA where they largely continued their work. His brother would have a different experience as a captive of the Americans.

On 4 June 1942 the experiment was ready. The first rocket-firing from a dived U-boat was successful. From a depth of 12 metres *U-511* succeeded in firing six rockets from the water at an angle of 45°. The flight path of the weapons did not exhibit any major ballistic deviations once they had passed through the water surface. Naturally, however, this new weapon was not yet effective enough to be used in action against the Allies. But it was obvious that the rockets possessed enormous future potential.

In the year 1944 another refinement to what had been the deck firing of the rockets was discussed. A towed container was considered that could house a large single rocket of V2 dimensions for firing at land targets. However, like many of Hitler's 'miracle weapons', the idea was never transformed into reality.

After release from the secret rocket experiments, Steinhoff carried out two patrols aboard *U-511*. On the first war patrol, to the Caribbean Sea, Steinhoff sank two tankers and damaged a third. However, his second war patrol ended without success as he had to abandon it on health grounds. After his return he was transferred to a new staff officer position.[109] After more than a year in this position, Steinhoff was returned to active duty and given command of *U-873* and it was here that the remaining crew from *U-604* met their new commander. This boat was a type IXD2 built by the Deschimag Werft in Bremen and placed into service on 1 March 1944.

After commissioning, the boat's path followed the normal pattern of each U-boat training for combat. After the UAG was successfully completed, the boat sailed to Kiel to the UAK. The UAK examinations started on 3 March 1944 and after two weeks, *U-873* moved onward to Swinemünde for flak firing exercises and from there on to Gotenhafen for torpedo shooting exercises.[110]

Afterward *U-873* travelled to Danzig where in the Holm Werft the engineless helicopter known as a 'Wagtail' (*Bachstelze*) was taken aboard. This was the Fokke Achgelis FA 330, known more correctly as a gyro-copter. This aircraft was operated by a surfaced U-boat, the forward speed of the U-boat used to generate enough lift beneath the copter's rotors to enable lift off. The copter was then towed by a cable like a kite. The towing height of the Bachstelze was about 120 metres. By this method the usual field of vision from a U-boat conning tower that allowed for a horizon of 8 kilometres could be substantially increased.

Kapitänleutnant Friedrich Steinhoff, commander of *U-873*.

The pilot of the Bachstelze was connected to the U-boat also by means of a rudimentary telephone. By this method the pilot could communicate with the lookouts and report any sighting. After the Bachstelze deployment was finished it could be retrieved by means of a winch which pulled in the towing cable and allowed the pilot to land his small gyrocopter on the same platform from where it departed. One of the substantial disadvantages, however, was that the copter had then to be broken down and stowed away in pressure-resistant cylinders before the boat could dive. Of course, this clear time would not be feasible during an aircraft attack and so the whole apparatus was only really suitable for use in relatively weakly patrolled waters such as the Indian Ocean.[III]

Also of interest is the training of the pilot. A crew member was posted to training near Frankfurt-am-Main in order to gain experience aboard the small machine. From Gdansk the boat was transferred to Hela for tactical training, where *U-873* collided with another boat, resulting in minor damage to oil tank number 3. Thus she had to go back to the Holm shipyard for twelve days before she could resume Agru Front exercises in Hela.

After completing these on 1 July 1944 *U-873* returned to the Deschimag Werft in Bremen, where the remainder of work required was completed. The diesel engines used to charge the batteries were removed, so that the batteries had to be charged solely by use of the propulsion diesel engines. Work was completed on oil tank number 1 in order to increase the additional fuel capacity. The upper deck in proximity to the bow was reduced in size in order to decrease submersion

Left: Preparation of the first rocket battery planned to be fired from the deck of a submerged U-boat. *Right*: The rocket launching from aboard the deck of *U-511*. The firing angle of 45° can be clearly seen in the photograph.(With kind permission of the Deutsche Museum Bild-Nr. 10509 and 10500)

time. The keel was loaded with mercury and optical glass by Zeiss Jena. Altogether 100 tons of additional cargo load was possible by using the keel area. Finally, a snorkel was fitted making it possible for *U-873* to spend extended periods of time submerged while still running on diesel engines. The snorkel allowed fresh air to be drawn in to feed the diesels and replenish the air in the boat, while exhaust gases could be expelled and all done at periscope depth.[112]

It was apparent that *U-873* was being converted into a dual purpose boat – torpedo and freight carrier.

On 30 July 1944 *U-873* lay in the Bremen shipyard when it was hit during an air raid. The bomb turned out to be a dud. It fell directly on the conning tower above the control room and killed a crewman, wounding three others. In order to repair this new damage *U-873* remained in the yards until the end of November when it finally put to sea and headed to Kiel for its first snorkel exercises.

The snorkel was both a blessing and a curse for the U-boat service. The boat speed while travelling submerged on diesels was reduced to four knots, otherwise the vibrations were too great for the snorkel mast, let alone the periscope which was supposed to be manned at all times. Without visual detection it would be possible for the enemy to close in on a submerged snorkelling U-boat as the hydrophone operator was nearly deafened by the combination of diesel engines and rushing water. It was a major benefit that the boat's batteries could be charged while remaining submerged, and the U-boat made one more step towards being a true submarine rather than a submersible still. Once the boat was switched to electric drive the speed dropped further lest the batteries be exhausted too rapidly. Due to the brief distances covered while travelling submerged, actual patrol lengths in the area of operations were also severely curtailed due to the length of

1 March 1944 — Commissioning of *U-873* (Steinhoff) in Bremen.

time it took to travel to and fro, all the while exhausting the food supplies carried aboard the boat. In the end, even the head of the snorkel could be detected by Allied centimetric radar.

In rough seas, use of the snorkel could be most unpleasant for the crew. If a wave washed over the snorkel head, a specially designed valve closed to prevent seawater entering the snorkel mast and ultimately the diesel engines. However, with engines still running, they required air and the necessary air was instead sucked from the interior of the boat. This created a terrible vacuum.

According to the statements of former crew members from *U-873*, these high-pressure fluctuations probably burst some men's ear drums. With others it produced nose bleeds and in one case at the end of December a man was even rendered unconscious.[113]

At the end of December 1944, *U-873* was taken to the shipyard in Stettin where the diesel compressors were exchanged and the bilge pumps numbers 1 and 3 were repaired.

A report from George Seitz (former Funkmaat aboard *U-873*):

In November 1944 the type IXD2 *U-873*, commanded by Kapitänleutnant Friedrich Steinhoff, lay in the Oderwerken in Stettin for final maintenance after completion of the tactical exercises. During one evening after the end of office hours, a large Maybach Limousine with a general's standard drove on to the pier. The driver stepped out and asked the sentry before the ship for the boat number and name of the commander. After he received this information, an army general and two civilians got out of the car.

In the meantime Kaptlt Steinhoff came on deck and joyfully welcomed the three gentlemen. Everyone then went into the officers' mess of the boat. We took the driver, an army Oberfeldwebel, into the *Unteroffizier* room, sitting on the lower bunks. We opened some drinks – Becks beer and schnapps. The radio operators controlled the record player and the night became very merry.

We then discovered who our visitors were. It was a General of the V-weapons, General Dr Dornberger, Werner von Braun and the commander's brother Dr Ernst Steinhoff from the V-weapon research station at Peenemünde.

At around midnight the general called out from the Officers' Mess 'Driver, to me!' The Oberfeldwebel leapt up immediately and bashed his head on the metal framework of the upper bunk. He nearly knocked himself out and sat straight back down again. Some minutes later there was another call: 'The driver to me!' We, however, did not let him get up and stand any more. Armed with youthful courage and fortified by drink and amidst much laughter from the U-room, Zentralemaat August Mohren from Aachen bent himself over backward and called in his Rheinish dialect: 'The jenneral is to come to us!' towards the Officers' Mess. The driver paled before our eyes in fright. After approximately one minute a smiling General Dornberger, with full glass in hand, followed by Werner von Braun and Dr Ernst Steinhoff came into the U-room to join us for a drink. One week later the crew of *U-873* were fetched by a Luftwaffe bus and driven to Peenemünde where we were guests in the casino.

On 6 January 1945 *U-873* was in Kiel loading freight for its outbound voyage. Even the supply of Becks beer was replenished, each bottle carefully rolled up in straw. The rumours were that the boat would be going to Penang (Malaya) or onward to Japan. A type IXD2 was indeed capable of completing this momentous voyage without refuelling, with its cruising range of 31,000 nautical miles. The boat sailed on 17 February, but only to head to Horten, Norway, in order to practise using the snorkel in an area designated by the Kriegsmarine for pre-combat training off the south-eastern Norwegian coastline. The boat reached its temporary base on 22 March after sailing mainly submerged. During the snorkelling exercises there was one unfortunate accident. When preparing to

The boat emblem for the type IX D2 boat
U-873.

surface Steinhoff ordered a survey with the listening gear but omitted the customary all-round look on his periscope. He deeming the area safe and *U-873* surfaced. However, they had managed to come up directly beneath a stationary type VIIC and again the boat suffered some collision damage. Oil tank number 6 was dented, the 37 mm flak disabled and the starboard number 7 diving tank severely dented as well.[114] The damage could not be repaired in Horten and so *U-873* was compelled to head on to Fredrikstadt where the shipyard had more extensive facilities. It took twelve days to repair the damage and then *U-873* went to Kristiansand where final preparations for the war patrol were undertaken.

Finally on 30 March 1945, *U-873* left harbour alongside another type IXC boat and one of the new type XXIII electro-boats. However, once more fate intervened and the weather was so bad that all three boats had to abort and return to harbour. Nonetheless on the last day of the month they all resailed and this time were successful. *U-873* proceeded on snorkel until 5 May 1945, heading via the Denmark route into the Atlantic and destined immediately for the Caribbean. That day received the radio notification that Dönitz had become the successor to the now dead Führer. The following day another message arrived, this one more profound and of extreme importance. It was the final instruction for his U-boat men from Grossadmiral Karl Dönitz, head of state and commander-in-chief of the Kriegsmarine:

My U-boat men!
Six years of U-boat warfare lies behind us. You have fought like lions.

A crushing material superiority has compressed us into a very narrow area. A continuation of the struggle is impossible from the bases that remain. U-boat men, unbroken in your warlike courage, you are laying down your arms after an heroic fight that knows no equal. In reverent memory we think of our comrades who have sealed their loyalty to the Führer and the Fatherland with their death. Comrades, maintain in the future your U-boat spirit with which you have fought at sea bravely and steadfastly during long years for the welfare of the Fatherland.
Long live Germany!

Your Grossadmiral.

On 7 May *U-873* received radioed instructions to begin its retreat to Norway and capitulation. But the officers aboard *U-873* were not willing to do so immediately and they debated their best course of action, keeping *U-873* on its original course. Two days later a radio message transmitted in the clear (uncoded) was received that stated that all U-boats in proximity to the American coastline should head toward American ports in order to surrender. To signal that the boat was indeed intending to surrender, a black flag should be attached to the periscope and flown in full view. Knowing that surrender was inevitable, Steinhoff ordered the destruction of all secret documents aboard *U-873*. On 11 May the order was given that *U-873* proceed to the closest American port. A few hours later screw noises were detected in the GHG, immediately identified as hostile destroyers. As *U-873* was submerged, Steinhoff faced the reality of his situation and immediately ordered the boat surfaced into the clear night, whereupon as soon as the water had cleared from the conning tower Steinhoff ordered un-encrypted messages transmitted to the approaching Americans. Since there was in fact no black flag available within the U-boat, the dark green curtain from Steinhoff's 'cabin' was used instead, flown from the conning tower.[115]

U-873 lay stopped as the enemy approached, the destroyer USS *Vance* illuminating the U-boat before coming near and despatching a boarding party to take over control of Steinhoff's boat. Georg Seitz remembered the arrival of the American boarding party:

> The prize crew sent over by the US destroyer were quite jumpy because the American sailors were not completely sure whether they were safe or whether our supposed surrender was a trap. First, none of the Americans seemed to speak German, though it soon turned out that there was a German-speaker among the boarding party. Instead they just stood and listened as the German crew talked among themselves. After only two days was I astonished when one of the American sailors asked me in a Mannheim dialect, 'Where are you from?' I answered, 'I am from Mannheim.' The American: 'You are from Mannheim itself?' Me: 'No, I am from Seggene [that is, Seckenheim, a suburb of Mannheim].' The American replied: 'Do you know the Hartmann's butcher's shop?' Me: 'Of course I know it.' The American: 'Every week I rode to that butcher's shop with a bicycle to take supplies. At the time my parents ran a butcher's supplies shop in the Seckenheimer Road.' I asked: 'Who are you?' To which he replied, 'My name is Werner Loeb and I emigrated with my parents to the USA before the outbreak of war. My father now works for a meat factory in Chicago and I volunteered for service in the US Navy and was headed for the war in

the Pacific.' I asked him, 'Why did you not speak to me until today in German, and why did you not act as interpreter with your good German?' Loeb replied, 'I did not have permission from my officer to speak with you until today, since we were concerned that you might submerge on us again and it may be a trap. Therefore my job was to listen to your conversations during the previous days.' Since then Werner Loeb and I have remained in contact and consider ourselves compatriots. In fact, mutual respect and a friendly attitude developed over the days that followed as we all lived closely together during the trip to America. Possibly the good German beer contributed a little to this as well, shared by ourselves and the Americans. Again and again we raised a glass to 'Peace!'

Eventually on 17 May 1945, *U-873* arrived in company with USS *Vance* at the American naval base at Portsmouth, New Hampshire. Of course, this also marked the arrival of the second half of Höltring's crew into American captivity. They were placed in the Portsmouth naval prison, which was actually a penitentiary. When the incarcerated crew looked and saw American convicts with chains on their feet they joked about whether or not they would also receive them and have to hustle this way and that in the strained way the convicts did.[116] However, the Germans were never shackled. But for their captain things in the American prison would end most tragically. According to official statements Friedrich Steinhoff committed suicide in his cell on 19 May 1945 by breaking his sunglasses and opening the arteries in his wrists with the shards of glass. Also, according to statements from available sources, the primary cause for this was the result of a heavy depression that had set over the commander, exacerbated by his incarceration. Naturally, there was much speculation regarding his suicide. Yet all of the rumours remain unconfirmed. Hence I wish only to note what can be officially supported by evidence. Kapitänleutnant Friedrich Steinhoff was buried with military honours in a military graveyard not far away, in Fort Devens, Massachusetts.

After a short stay by the remainder of the crew in the Charles Street Prison, Boston, they were eventually sent to various American prisoner-of-war camps, the thirteen men of Höltring's old crew divided among them. However, they were never reunited in any of these camps with the nine survivors that had been taken prisoner after the sinking of *U-185* on 24 August 1943. And so here, the history of *U-604* finally ends.

Postscript

Altogether *U-604* spent 179 days on war patrols until 11 August 1943 when the boat was scuttled by its crew. If one considers, however, that in the year 1942 the average life expectancy of a German U-boat as speculated by the Allies was only 62 days, then *U-604* outlived this prognosis by a factor of 2.89. Whether this was due to the prudent nature in which Höltring handled his boat, or simply good luck, will forever remain conjectural.

U-604 sank 0.2614 per cent of the entire ship tonnage destroyed by Axis powers during World War II. Starting with *U-604*'s first day at sea on active duty to the final day of existence during its sixth war patrol, 206 German U-boats were lost to the enemy. From *U-604*, 16 men remain at sea.

From the six ships sunk by *U-604* there were 743 men aboard. Only 231 were saved, for the remaining 512 people help came too late.

U-604 sank the following ships:

1 *Abbekerk*	25.08.1942	9.489 BRT
2 *Anglo Maersk*	27.10.1942	7.705 BRT
3 *Baron Vernon*	30.10.1942	3.642 BRT
4 *President Doumer*	30.10.1942	11.899 BRT
5 *Coamo*	02.12.1942	7.057 BRT
6 *Stockport*	23.02.1943	1.683 BRT
Total tonnage:		41.474 BRT

Reunions of the Crew
In the years following the experiences aboard *U-604* the crew of the boat always remained connected. The former crew met annually at 'boat meetings'. At one of these in the 1980s even the former commander of *U-172*, Carl Emmermann, was present. As a gesture to acknowledge their gratitude *U-604*'s clock was presented to him; it had been dismantled in 1943 by a crew member before the

boat was scuttled and sank forever into the depths.

The last boat meeting took place in 2005. It is amazing how the comradeship of the crew remained intact after decades. The life-threatening experiences of the boat's war patrols in the Atlantic had merged them into a strongly linked community. Such solidarity can only be achieved during extreme situations in life. In this case it was the cooperation of the crew of a U-boat living in constant mortal danger. Everybody had to be able to rely on everybody else. The error of one individual could have endangered the survival of all. That is probably the reason for the lifelong friendships of the former crew members of Höltring's boat *U-604*. This deep comradeship and togetherness can be seen in a moving comment made by the former Obermaschinenmaat (First Zentralemaat) aboard *U-604*:

> When the boat left the shelter wall and steered on electric motors in the direction of the port exit on its way to a new war patrol, all military routines were left ashore. From that moment we were all just human beings together.

Words from Herr Georg Seitz, former Oberfunkmaat on U-604

> We are no longer many and daily become fewer,
>   we U-boat men of the Second World War.
> Faithful to our military oath we are driven out time and time again
>   into the icy storms of the North Atlantic as well as into the tropical
>   seas under the sign of the Southern Cross.
> After weeks of service at sea together with reliable comrades, in our
> hearts there is always the hope of a happy homecoming!

The Emblems of U-604

During World War II it was very common for U-boats to adorn their conning towers with some form of symbol to bring the boat luck. Generally they were chosen by the crew and referred to something from either the boat's history or the commander's.

The tower emblems of some of the better-known U-boats became famous throughout Germany. Occasionally, if a captain who had been successful in action was promoted to the role of flotilla commander, he took with him his emblem which then became that of all of the flotilla's boats as was the case for the 9th U-Flotilla. These flotilla emblems often lay side by side with more personal markings. For example, the first emblem chosen for *U-604* was a dolphin that had dived into the waves. This referred to the fact that Höltring had served in the naval aviation arm before transferring to U-boat service, so the dolphin represented both air and water. At the conclusion of its first war patrol, *U-604* added the 'laughing sawfish' of the 9th U-Flotilla, which in turn had come into use after Lehmann-Willenbrock moved ashore from his command of *U-96* where the emblem had originated.

The sawfish emblem came about almost by accident aboard *U-96*. Although Lehmann-Willenbrock wanted a symbol for his boat, neither he nor his crew

Left: *U-604*'s first emblem. *Right*: The second symbol for *U-604*; emblem of the 9th U-Flotilla

177

could decide on a picture until a crew member saw the sawfish cartoon inside a magazine. Drawn by the cartoonist Kossatz, it was swiftly adopted and painted on the conning tower, originally in green rather than the black that has since become a popular version.

On 1 February 1942 Lehmann-Willenbrock became commander of the 9th U-flotilla and so the laughing sawfish became the flotilla emblem, applied to all boats including *U-604*. It was also worn as a metal badge on the side of most crewmen's service caps.

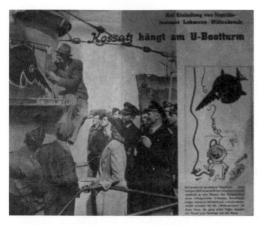

Above, left: Newspaper article relating to the laughing sawfish symbol adopted by *U-96*. On the right is the original advertisement that featured the illustration, and on the left a propaganda photograph of the artist Kossatz appearing to paint the emblem on the tower of *U-96*. In fact the symbol had already been applied; the picture was for propaganda purposes only. *Above right*: Lehmann-Willenbrock ending a patrol of *U-96* in Saint-Nazaire. *Left*: *U-96* with the sawfish emblem.

List of Crewmen of U-604

Wolfgang Pöschel, 1 WO Leutnant zur See: killed as commander of *U-422* on 4 October 1943.

Siegfried von Rothkirch und Panthen, 1 WO Leutnant zur See, became commander of *U-717*.

Hans Jürgen Stahmer, 1 WO, killed as commander of *U-354* on 24 August 1943.

Frank Aschmann, 1 WO and Oberleutnant zur See, killed on 30 July 1943 aboard *U-604*.

Jürgensen, 2 WO Leutnant der Reserve, posted from *U-604*.

Dr. v. Hermann Bothmer, 2 WO and Oberleutnant zur See, survived the sinking of *U-185* on 24 August 1943 and held in American captivity.

Helmut Jürgens, Oberleutnant Ingenieur, Leitender Ingenieur, surrendered with *U-873* taken prisoner by the Americans.

Stumpf, Fähnrich, posted from *U-604*.

Herbert Kühn, Oberleutnant zur See der Reserve Propaganda Kompanie, A reported that only accompanied *U-604* on its sixth patrol. After this patrol posted elsewhere.

Albert Finster, Obersteuermann and 3 WO, surrendered with *U-873* and held in American captivity.

Walter Aloe, Obermaschinist (E-Anlage), posted from *U-604*.

Gerhard Beugholz, Obermaschinist (E-Maschine), killed on *U-185* on 24 August 1943.

Wilhelm Schiffer, Obermaschinist (Diesel), surrendered with *U-873* and held in American captivity.

Helmut Altmann, Oberbootsmaat seemann no. 1, killed aboard *U-185* on 24 August 1943.

Peter Binnefeld, Oberbootsmaat seemann no. 2, surrendered with *U-873* and held in American captivity.

Herbert Lurz, Bootsmaat seemann no. 3, killed aboard *U-604* on 30 July 1943.

Ernst Schnede, Torpedo Mech. Maat, killed aboard *U-185* on 24 August 1943.

Alfred Dombrowsky, Obermaschinenmaat (Diesel), posted from *U-604*.

Berry Golz, Obermaschinenmaat (E-Anlage), posted from *U-604*.

Adolf Helsper, Obermaschinenmaat (Diesel), killed aboard *U-185* on 24 August 1943.

Fred Fröde, Maschinenmaat (Diesel), classified as unfit for U-boat service after *U-604*'s last war patrol and posted elsewhere.

Fritz Wagenführ, Maschinenmaat (Second Zentralemaat), survived the sinking of *U-185* on 24 August 1943 and held in American captivity.

Ernst Winter, Obermaschinenmaat (E-Maschine), survived the sinking of *U-185* on 24 August 1943 and held in American captivity.

Walter Ortwein, Maschinenmaat (E-Maschine), surrendered with *U-873* and held in American captivity.

Gerhard Giese, Oberfunkmaat, transferred from *U-604*.

Horst Keller, Funkmaat, killed aboard *U-185* on 24 August 1943.

Georg Seitz, Funkmaat, surrendered with *U-873* and held in American captivity.

Fritz Niebling, Funkmaat, transferred from *U-604*.

Robert Marquardt, Obermaschinenmaat (First Zentralemaat), after *U-604*'s last war patrol transferred to the AG Weser shipyard as instructor.

Heinrich Reiblich, Torpedo Mech. Obergefreiter, surrendered with *U-873* and held in American captivity.

Walter Nieswand, Torpedo Mech. Obergefreiter, survived the sinking of *U-185* on 24 August 1943 and held in American captivity.

Richard Opitz, Matrose Obergefreiter, killed on *U-185* on 24 August 1943.

Werner Schulz, Matrose Obergefreiter, killed *U-185* on 24 August 1943.

Ferdinand Bibo, Matrose Obergefreiter (cook), killed on *U-185* on 24 August 1943.

Horst Gebauer, Matrose Obergefreiter, transferred from *U-604* after final war patrol.

Heinz Trommer, Maschinen Obergefreiter, survived the sinking of *U-185* on 24 August 1943 and held in American captivity.

Horst Ehlert, Maschinen Obergefreiter, survived the sinking of *U-185* on 24 August 1943 and held in American captivity.

Rudolf Rotthner, Maschinen Obergefreiter, killed on *U-185* on 24 August 1943.

Karl Strauch, Maschinen Hauptgefreiter, killed on *U-185* on 24 August 1943.

Peter Seipel, Maschinen Obergefreiter, reassigned to further training course after the final war patrol of *U-604*.

Ernst Werner, Maschinen Obergefreiter, reassigned to training course after the final war patrol of *U-604*.

Erwin Klawien, Maschinen Obergefreiter reassigned to training course after the final war patrol of *U-604*.

Heinz Müller, Funkobergefreiter reassigned to training course after the final war patrol of *U-604*.

Walter Lux, Funkobergefreiter, killed on *U-185* on 24 August 1943.

Ewald Anschütz, Torp. Mech. Gefreiter, surrendered with *U-873* and held in American captivity.

Paul Bellmann, Torp. Mech.Gefreiter, killed on *U-185* on 24 August 1943.

Werner Eismann, Matrose Gefreiter, survived the sinking of *U-185* on 24 August 1943 and held in American captivity.

Werner Beher, Matrose Obergefreiter (Gefechtsrudergänger) Survived the sinking of *U-185* on 24 August 1943 and held in American captivity.

Wilhelm Schnitte, Matrose Gefreiter, killed on *U-185* on 24 August 1943.

Eduard Rogowski, Matrose Obergefreiter, surrendered with *U-873* and held in American captivity.

Günter Alrutz, Matrose Obergefreiter, after the final War Patrol by *U-604*, reassigned to further training course.

Otto Schreckenbach, Maschinen Obergefreiter, surrendered with *U-873* and held in American captivity.

Heinz Lüttges, Maschinen Obergefreiter, survived the sinking of *U-185* on 24 August 1943 and held in American captivity.

Ernst Schröter, Maschinen Obergefreiter, surrendered with *U-873* and held in American captivity.

Hugo Schuhmacher, Maschinen Obergefreiter,after the final War Patrol by *U-604*, reassigned to further training course.

Gerhard Krimmling, Maschinen Gefreiter, survived the sinking of *U-185* on 24 August 1943 and held in American captivity.

Hans Beck, Maschinen Obergefreiter, surrendered with *U-873* and held in American captivity.

Notes

1   Prof. Dr Jürgen Rohwer, *Eine Chronik in Bildern*, Oldenburg Gerhard Stalling Verlag (1962), pp 93–6.
2   Harald Bendert, *U-Boote im Duell*, Hamburg, E.S. Mittler und Sohn (1996), pp. 112–13.
3   David Miller, *U-Boote bis 1945*, Stuttgart, Motorbuchverlag (2000), p. 134–5.
4   Jak Mallmann Showell, *Die U-Boot-Waffe*, Stuttgart, Motorbuch Verlag (2001), p. 10.
5   Interview with Georg Seitz, former Funkmaat aboard *U-604*, December 2007.
6   Telephone interview with Dr Hess, former commander of *U-995*, 1998.
7   Interview with Georg Seitz, former Funkmaat aboard *U-604*, 1999.
8   Telephone interview with Robert Marquardt, former 1st Zentralemaat aboard *U-604*, December 2007.
9   Such provocative statistics printed on handbills and dropped by Allied aircraft over the German submarine bases along the French Atlantic coast as a part of the propaganda war. The attempt to erode the morale and confidence of the U-boat was ultimately unsuccessful, although the empty berths within the U-boat bunkers spoke loudly enough of Germany's losses at sea.
10   V. E. Tarrant, *Kurs West: Die deutschen U-Boot-Offensiven 1914–1945*, Stuttgart, Motorbuch Verlag (1998), p. 116.
11   Clay Blair, *Der U-Boot-Krieg: Die Gejagten 1942–1945*, München, Wilhelm Heyne Verlag (1998), appendix 2.
12   Tarrant, *Kurs West,* p. 151.
13   Jürgen Rohwer, *Der Krieg zur See*, Gräfelfing bei München, Urbes Verlag (1992), p. 105.
14   Miller, *U-Boote bis 1945*, p. 86.
15   Lawrence Paterson, *U564 auf Feindfahrt*, Stuttgart, Motorbuch Verlag (2005), p. 58.
16   Jürgen Rohwer and G. Hümmelchen, *Chronik des Seekrieges 1939–1945*, Oldenburg and Hamburg, Hersching (1968), p. 42.
17   Jürgen Rohwer, *Chronology of the War at Sea 1939–1945*, London, Chatham Publishing (1999), p. 192.
18   Date taken from Landesbibliothek Stuttgart (http://www.wlb-stuttgart.de).
19   Interview with Hermann Friedrich, former E-Maschinist aboard *U-96*, 1 November 2000.
20   Date taken from Landesbibliothek Stuttgart (http://www.wlb-stuttgart.de).
21   Miller, *U-Boote bis 1945*, p. 108 and interview with Georg Seitz.
22   Blair, *Der U-Boot-Krieg,* appendix 2.
23   Interview with Herr Weigel, former crewman aboard *U-288*, *U-733* and *U-3028*, 28 August 2000.

24   Date taken from Landesbibliothek Stuttgart (http://www.wlb-stuttgart.de).

25   Rohwer, *Chronology of the War at Sea 1939–1945*, p. 206.

26   Paterson, *U564 auf Feindfahrt*, p. 171.

27   Blair, *Der U-Boot-Krieg*, p. 106.

28   Jürgen Rohwer, *Axis Submarine Successes of World War Two*, London, Greenhill Books (1999),
     p. 130.

29   Ibid., p. 131.

30   Ibid.

31   Ibid., pp. 129–31.

32   Tarrant, *Kurs West*, pp. 151–3.

33   This particular quote attributed to Godt features in the book by David Miller. However, there has been some doubt as to whether this is in fact based on a real point of view expressed by Godt. Nonetheless, there was often less training as a result of a shortage of trained men at the front, the desire to get more boats into action and the ever increasing supply of new technology, resulting in what could be seen as curtailed training.

34   Blair, *Der U-Boot-Krieg*, appendix 2.

35   Tarrant, *Kurs West*, p. 153.

36   Ibid., p. 139.

37   *The Prosecution against the Main War Criminals Before the International Military Court*, Nürnberg (1947), vol. 8, p. 309 and War Diary from BdU.

38   Email interview with Captain Henry Helgesen, 2008.

39   Blair, *Der U-Boot-Krieg*, appendix 2.

40   Tarrant, *Kurs West*, pp. 157 and 160.

41   Blair, *Der U-Boot-Krieg*, pp. 42–3.

42   Ibid., p. 237.

43   Ibid., p. 238.

44   Rohwer, *Chronology of the War at Sea 1939–1945*, p. 232.

45   Blair, *Der U-Boot-Krieg*, p. 238.

46   Rohwer and Hümmelchen, *Chronik des Seekrieges 1939–1945*, p. 330.

47   Rohwer, *Chronology of the War at Sea 1939–1945*, p. 232

48   Blair, *Der U-Boot-Krieg*, p. 239.

49   Rohwer, *Axis Submarine Successes of World War Two*, p. 150.

50   In fact *U-92* had sunk the 9,990-ton British ship *Empire Trade*, ibid.

51   Blair, *Der U-Boot-Krieg*, p. 239.

52   Rohwer, *Axis Submarine Successes of World War Two*, p. 150.

53   Blair, *Der U-Boot-Krieg*, p. 240 and Op-16-Z: Report on the interrogation of survivors from *U-606*.

54   John M. Waters, *Bloody Winter*, New York, Van Nostrand (1967).

55   Rohwer, *Axis Submarine Successes of World War Two*, p. 151.

56   Ibid., p. 152.

57   Paper, Antisubmarine action by aircraft ic/dent no. 2595.

58   Rohwer, *Axis Submarine Successes of World War Two*, p. 150-2.

59   Blair, *Der U-Boot-Krieg*, appendix 2.

60   Tarrant, *Kurs West*, pp. 157 and 160.

61   Telephone interview with Herr Robert Marquardt, former first Zentralemaat aboard *U-604*. January 2008.

62   Blair, *Der U-Boot-Krieg*, appendix 2.

Notes

63   Gudrun Strüber, *Blaue Jungs! Grüne Jungs?,* Bilshausen, Fabuloso-Verlag (2002), p. 44.
64   Tarrant, *Kurs West*, p. 160.
65   Blair, *Der U-Boot-Krieg*, appendix 2.
66   Tarrant, *Kurs West*, p. 161.
67   Ibid., after 'The Defeat of the Enemy Attack on Shipping' p. 97.
68   Strüber, *Blaue Jungs! Grüne Jungs?*, p. 44.
69   Interview with Georg Seitz, former Funkmaat aboard *U-604*, November 2007.
70   Rohwer, *Der Krieg zur See*, p. 146.
71   Blair, *Der U-Boot-Krieg*, appendix 2.
72   Interview with Georg Seitz, former Funkmaat aboard *U-604*, 2001.
73   Blair, *Der U-Boot-Krieg*, p. 456.
74   Ibid., p. 476 and Op-16-Z: Report on the interrogation of the survivors from *U-487*.
75   Alan C. Carey, *Galloping Ghosts of the Brazilian Coast*, New York, iUniverse Inc. (2004), p.52.
76   Ibid., p. 55 and Op-16-Z: Report on the survivors from *U-662*.
77   Op-16-Z: Report on interrogation of the survivors from *U-614* and *U-185*.
78   Ibid.
79   Carey, *Galloping Ghosts*, p. 61 and Op-16-Z Report.
80   Interview with Herr Georg Seitz,former Funkmaat aboard *U-604*, about 1999.
81   Report of antisubmarine action by aircraft, Unit VB-129, Report no. 1, no. 3893.
82   Carey, *Galloping Ghosts*, p. 62.
83   Interview with Herr Georg Seitz,former Funkmaat aboard *U-604*, 1999.
84   Telephone interview with Herr Robert Marquardt, former first Zentralemaat aboard *U-604*. January 2008.
85   Interview with Herr Georg Seitz, former Funkmaat aboard *U-604*, 2003
86   Op-16-Z: Report.
87   Carey, *Galloping Ghosts*, p. 63.
88   Blair, *Der U-Boot-Krieg*, p. 443 and Report of antisubmarine action by aircraft number 3892.
89   Rohwer, *Axis Submarine Successes of World War Two*, p. 169.
90   Report of antisubmarine action by aircraft, Unit VB–107, Report no. 7, no. 01886.
91   Op-16-Z: Report.
92   Carey, *Galloping Ghosts*, p. 73.
93   Blair, *Der U-Boot-Krieg*, p. 445.
94   Carey, *Galloping Ghosts*, p. 126.
95   Interview with Herr Georg Seitz, former Funkmaat aboard *U-604*, 1999.
96   Telephone interview with Herr Ernst Winter, former Obermaschinenmaat aboard *U-604*, 2007.
97   Telephone interview with Herr Robert Marquardt, former first Zentralemaat aboard *U-604*, December 2007.
98   Blair, *Der U-Boot-Krieg*, p. 480.
99   John F. White: U-Boot Tanker, 1941–1945, Koehler 1998 p. 163.
100 Op-16-Z: Report.
101 The letter is also published by Gudrun Strüber in her book *Blaue Jungs! Grüne Jungs?*, p. 176.
102 Ibid., p. 179.
103 Interview with Herr Georg Seitz, former Funkmaat aboard *U-604*, 2001.
104 Report of antisubmarine action by aircraft, number 8/43, UC1.
105 These already published events could not be verified by Herr Seitz.

106 Interview with Herr Georg Seitz, former Funkmaat aboard *U-604* and *U-873*, 2007.
107 Telephone interview with Herr Robert Marquardt, former first Zentralemaat aboard *U-604*, December 2007.
108 Ibid.
109 Op-16-Z: Report.
110 Ibid.,
111 Interview with Georg Seitz, former Oberfunkmaat aboard *U-873*, 1999.
112 Op-16-Z: Report.
113 Interview with Georg Seitz, former Oberfunkmaat aboard *U-873*, 1999.
114 Op-16-Z: Report.
115 Interview with Georg Seitz, former Oberfunkmaat aboard *U-873*, 1999.
116 Ibid.

References

Archives

Bibliothek für Zeitgeschichte in der Württembergische Landesbibliothek/Marinearchiv Konrad-
    Adenauer-Str. 8, D-70173 Stuttgart

Bundesarchiv–Militärarchiv, Freiburg, Wiesentalstraße 10, 79115 Freiburg

Deutsches U-Boot-Museum, Archiv für Internationale Unterwasserfahrt, Bahnhofstraße 57,
    27478 Cuxhaven Altenbruch

Experts who assisted with specific questions

Dr Axel Niestlé and Dr Peter Schenk (identification of photographs)

Ernst Winter, Georg Seitz and Robert Marquardt (former crew members of *U-604*)

Heinz Trompelt (former crew member of *U-172*)

Hermann Friedrich (former crew member of *U-96*)

Unpublished Sources: documents were provided by

Georg Seitz (former Funkmaat aboard *U-604*)

Ernst Winter (former Obermaschinenmaat aboard *U-604*)

Peter Binnefeld (son of a crewman from *U-604*)

Captain Jerry Mason

Bernhard Schlummer

Gudrun Strüber (daughter of a crewman from *U-604*)

Sketches, article, reports and war diaries:

Reports of Antisubmarine Action by Aircraft:

    Unit VC-13, USS *Core* Unit Report No. 5, Incident no. 4082

    Unit VB–107, Report no. 7, no. 01886

    Unit VB–107, Report no. 1, no. 369/

    Unit VB-127, Report No. 1, Incident no. 3892

    Unit VB-129: Report no. 1 *Base of Operation: Bahia, Brazil*, incident no. 3893

    Incident no. 2595

    United States Atlantic Fleet, Air Force Bombing Squadron 129

Op-16-Z: Navy Department, Office of the Chief of Naval Operations, Washington: Documents
    relating the interrogation of survivors from *U-128*, *U-185*, *U-487*, *U-591*, *U-604*, *U-606*, *U-
    662* and *U-873*

War diaries of U-boats and their commanders

War diary of *U-604* (Bundesarchiv RM 98/206)

War diary of *U-172*

References

Verband Deutscher U-Boot-Fahrer e.V.: Schaltung Küste: Ehemals monatlich erscheinendes Infoblatt (Association of German U-boat driver eV: Coastal Circuit: Formerly monthly information sheet)

Photograph sources: libraries
Air Force Historical Research Agency, 600 Chennault Circle, BLDG 1405, Maxwell AFB, AL36112-6424
Bibliothek für Zeitgeschichte in der Württembergische Landesbibliothek / Marinearchiv, Konrad-Adenauer-Str. 8, D-70173 Stuttgart, Germany
Blohm & Voss GmbH / Öffentlichkeitsarbeit
Bundesarchiv–Militärarchiv, Freiburg, Wiesentalstraße 10, 79115 Freiburg, Germany
Deutsches Museum / Bildstelle, Museumsinsel 1, 80306 München, Germany
National Archives & Records Administration Still Picture, Reference Team - RMB, 8601 Adelphi Road Room 5360, College Park, MD 20740-6001
Mit freundlicher Genehmigung des National Archives & Records, Administration Still Picture Reference Team - RMB, 8601 Adelphi Road Room 5360, College Park, MD 20740-6001
Thyssen Krupp Marine Systems AG, Hermann Blohm Straße 3, 20457 Hamburg, Germany
Ullstein Bild, Axel – Springer – Straße 65, 10888 Berlin

Photograph sources: private collections
Captain Henry Helgensen; Captain Jerry Mason; Bernhard Schlummer; Christian Prag; Ernst Winter (former Obermaschinenmaat from *U-604*); Georg Seitz (former Funkmaat from *U-604*); H. Friedrich (former crewman from *U-96*); Peter Binnefeld (son of *U-604* crewman); Richard A. Wilson; Robert F. Sumrall; Frau von Voss

In some cases the photographer unfortunately could not be identified. Please contact the author regarding any questions on this matter.

Internet:
http://www.bundesarchiv.de
http://www.es-conseil.fr/pramona/ pdtdoumer.htm
http://www.uboat.net
http://www.uboatarchive.net
http://www.uboatarchive.net
http://www.ubootwaffe.net

http://www.wikipedia.org
http://www.warsailors.com
http://www.wlb-stuttgart.de
http://afhra.maxwell.af.mil/
http://www.archives.gov/
http://www.navytorpedo.com

Books
Bagnasco, Erminio *U-Boote im 2. Weltkrieg* Motorbuchverlag, Stuttgart (1997)
Bendert, Harald *U-Boote im Duell* E. S. Mittler & Sohn GmbH (1996)
Blair, Clay *Der U-Boot-Krieg 'Die Gejagten'* Heyne (1999)
Blair, Clay *Der U-Boot-Krieg 'Die Jäger'* Heyne (1996)
Brennecke, Jochen *Jäger Gejagte 1939–1945* Koehler Verlagsgesellschaft (1956)
Buchheim, Lothar-Günther *Die U-Boot-Fahrer* Blank (2005)
Buchheim, Lothar-Günther *U-Boot-Krieg* Piper (np) (1976)
Buchheim, Lothar-Günther *Zu Tode gesiegt* Piper (np) (2001)
Busch, Rainer and Hans-Joachim Röll *Der U-Boot-Krieg 1939–1945, Bd.1, Die deutschen U-Boot-Kommandanten* Mittler & Sohn (2000)
Busch, Rainer and Hans-Joachim Röll *Der U-Boot-Krieg 1939-1945, Bd.2, Der U-Boot-Bau auf deutschen Werften von 1935 bis 1945* Mittler & Sohn (1997)

References

Busch, Rainer and Hans-Joachim Röll *Der U-Boot-Krieg 1939-1945, Bd.3, Der U-Boot-Krieg 1939-1945, Deutsche U-Boot-Erfolge von September 1939 bis Mai 1945* Mittler & Sohn (2001)

Busch, Rainer and Hans Joachim Röll *Die Deutschen U-Boot-Kommandanten* E. S. Mittler & Sohn Hamburg, Berlin (1996)

Carey, Alan C. *Galloping Ghosts of the Brazilian Coast* (Universe, Inc.)

Deutscher, Harald *So war der U-Boot* Krieg Busch Heimatverlag, Bielefeld 1952

Dönitz, Karl *Zehn Jahre und zwanzig Tage. Erinnerungen 1935–1945* Bernard & Graefe Verlag (1997)

Dornberger Walter *Peenemünde: Die Geschichte der V-Waffen* Ullstein

Hague, Arnold *The Allied Convoy System, 1939-1945* Chatham Publishing. London (2003)

Herzog, Bodo *U-Boote im Einsatz* Podzun Verlag, Dorheim (1970)

Herzog, Bodo *60 Jahre Deutsche Uboote 1906–1966* Verlag: J. F. Lehmanns Verlag, München (nd)

Högel, Georg *Embleme, Wappen, Malings deutscher U-Boote 1939–1945* Koehlers Verlagsgesellschaft

Kurowski, Franz *Jäger der sieben Meere* Motorbuchverlag 2. Auflage (1998)

Koop, Gerhard *Kampf und Untergang der Deutschen U-Boot-Waffe* (1998) Bernhard & Graefe Verlag

Merk, Otto *Damals in Peenemünde* Gerhard Stalling Verlag (1963)

Miller, David *Deutsche U-Boote bis 1945* Motorbuchverlag (2000)

Möller, Eberhard *Kurs Atlantik* Motorbuch Verlag, Stuttgart

The Prosecution Against The Main War Criminals before the International Military Court, Nuremberg 1947

Padfield, Peter *Dönitz: Des Teufels Admiral* Ullstein, Berlin (1984)

Paterson, Lawrence *U-564 auf Feindfahrt* Motorbuch Verlag, Stuttgart

Plottke, Herbert *Fächer Los* U-172 *im Einsatz* (Podzun Pallas)

Rahn, Werner and Gerhard Schreiber *Kriegstagebuch der Seekriegsleitung 1939–1945* Mittler & Sohn

Ritschel, Herbert *Kriegstagebücher deutscher U-Boote 1939-1945, Band 5, KTB: U-171–U-222* Eigenverlag, Korntal (1997–2004)

Rössler, Eberhard *Die Torpedos der deutschen U-Boote: Entwicklung, Herstellung und Eigenschaften der deutschen Marine-Torpedos* Mittler & Sohn

Rössler, Eberhard *Die Geschichte des deutschen U-Bootbaus* Bernhard & Graefe Verlag (1996)

Roskill, S. W. *War at Sea 1939-45: Defensive* vol. 1 Naval & Military Press Ltd ISBN 978-1843428039

Rohwer, Jürgen *Axis Submarine Successes of World War Two* Greenhill Books, London

Rohwer, Jürgen *Chronology of the War At Sea 1939–1945* Chatham Publishing, London (2005)

Rohwer, Jürgen and G. Hümmelchen *Chronik des Seekrieges 1939–1945* Manfred Pawlak Verlagsgesellschaft mbH, Herrsching

Rohwer, Jürgen *Der Krieg zur See 1939–1945* Urbes (1992)

Rohwer, Jürgen *Geleitzugschlachten im März 1943: Führungsprobleme im Höhepunkt d. Schlacht im Atlantik* Motorbuch Verlag, Stuttgart (1975)

Rohwer, Jürgen *U-Boote. Eine Chronik in Bildern* Gerhard Stalling Verlag, Oldenburg (1962)

Showell, Jak Mallmann *Die U-Boot-Waffe* Motorbuchverlag (2001)

Strüber, Gudrun *Blaue Jungs, Grüne Jungs* Fabuloso Verlag) (2002)

Tarrant, V. E. *Kurs West* Motorbuchverlag, Stuttgart (1998)

Waters, John M. *Blutiger Winter* Welsermühl, München (1970)

White, John F. *U-Boot Tanker 1941–1945* 1998 Koehler Verlagsgesellschaft Hamburg

Williams, Kathleen Broome *Secret Weapon: US High-Frequency Direction Finding in the Battle of the Atlantic* Naval Institute Press (December 1996)

Index

Index of Ships

Index